READER'S DIGEST
WAR STORIES

READER'S DIGEST
WAR STORIES

Daring first-hand accounts of World War II
from the magazine archives

PUBLISHED BY
The Reader's Digest Association, Inc.
London • New York • Sydney • Montreal

Contents

FOREWORD

As someone who has always taken a close interest in military history I am naturally fascinated by the great sweep of major events: the critical decisions; the impact of economies, technology and population levels; the opportunities seized or missed; and of course the vagaries of chance. All of these play a key part in shaping history and thereby determining our present. And as someone who has commanded military forces at the strategic level, I am only too aware of the importance of these grand themes. But I am also conscious that they form only part of the story. Even the largest military force is made up of individuals, and how each one of them behaves determines the capacity and potential of the whole. Put simply, the commitment, determination and courage of individuals underpin the effectiveness of the organisations to which they belong.

So if we are to understand history it is no good just looking at key dates and major events. We must understand the people who took part in them: how they felt, how they thought, and how they behaved. Only then does the past come alive in a way that enables us to understand it and relate to it. Only then does history tell us something meaningful about who we are and where we come from. So I am delighted that *Reader's Digest* has brought together these articles on World War II. They include first-person accounts of courage, of endurance, of initiative, and of humour in the darkest circumstances. They are not just fascinating stories though; they also illustrate a fundamental tenet of military success: it is founded on ordinary people doing extraordinary things in the face of adversity. This splendid book is a testament not just to the individuals involved, but to that enduring truth.

Air Chief Marshal The Lord Stirrup
June 2012

INTRODUCTION

eader's Digest has always had a special association with war. Its founder, DeWitt Wallace, came up with the idea for the magazine while he was convalescing, having been pumped full of shrapnel during World War I. He enjoyed reading so many publications while lying on his sickbed that he wanted to find a way of condensing them so that he—and, as it turned out, millions of others—could continue to enjoy them post-recovery. In 1922, the first issue of what was to become a global publishing phenomenon was launched. There are now 50 editions around the world in 21 languages.

Our own UK version—the first international edition—was launched with unfortunate timing in March 1938. Undaunted by the outbreak of World War II, we published throughout—smaller, thinner and on poorer quality paper, yes, but published nonetheless. Those issues, and the stories of the war featured in the following decades, offer a unique and fascinating insight into wartime life.

Some of the most poignant and revealing articles come from readers themselves—winners of the *Reader's Digest* "First Person" Award—and it is those articles that form a large part of this book. The award was given for "true and hitherto unpublished" stories that were "adventurous, humorous, dramatic or inspirational" and World War II provided a rich seam.

In the early years of the magazine a great deal of the content came from the US edition. Consequently the stories featured here—many from US servicemen—paint a truly global picture of the war. From Japanese POW camps to French fields; the Burmese jungle to the Philippine Sea, there are accounts from airmen, seamen, soldiers and even spies.

Their stories unfold in clear, no-nonsense prose, recounted, no doubt with a heavily stiffened upper lip. "Being a 'Tail-End Charlie' was rated by the RAF a 'hazardous occupation'" writes former rear-gunner Nicholas Stephen Alkemade, of his leap from a burning Lancaster at 18,000 feet—

without a parachute! In *Trapped!* a young sailor awaits rescue deep below decks in a sinking ship. "I passed out again, then gradually became aware of the chaplain's voice … Then, with a sickening jolt, I realized what the chaplain was doing. He was reading my funeral service!" The simple telling belies the horrors of their experiences.

Then there are the profiles of key war figures—from *Monty, the People's General* to *Mark, the War-Dog Hero*. These accounts serve as a reminder of just what it took to fight—and win.

But—in true *Reader's Digest* style, where laughter really is the best medicine—an element of humour is never far away. *My Ride on a Torpedo*, a feature illustrated with an unforgettable image of a young ship's commander astride a 24-foot weapon, is *Boy's Own* drama at its best! *The Affair of the Vanishing Pesos* is a tense but ultimately triumphant account of how a group of American divers outwitted their captors when they were put to work salvaging silver in the Japanese-occupied Philippines in 1944. And on page 8, the late Harry Secombe offers a completely different take on war—and *Reader's Digest*—as a young (and somewhat light-fingered) conscript.

But for all the entertaining anecdotes, there's a more serious underlying agenda. In *I Shot Down Yamamoto*, Thomas Lanphier recalls the death of his brother. "As I stood with my family at Charlie's funeral, I realized more than ever the tragedy and futility of war. How ironic, I thought, that I should shoot down Admiral Yamamoto over Kahili—and that Charlie should be shot down at virtually the same spot. I wondered sadly if mankind, which had reasoned its way to the atom, might not one day reason its way to a true peace."

For that sentiment alone, the stories of war need telling and retelling for years to come.

Gill Hudson
Reader's Digest *magazine Editor-in-Chief*
June 2012

Reading for Pleasure

BY HARRY SECOMBE

(Alias Ned Seagoon of the Goon Show; star comedian of radio, television and variety)

Back in 1942, when I was unable to dodge the call-up any longer, I found myself, as it were, backed into a corner. A corner of the platform at Waterloo Station. The time: just as a recruit-hungry train pulled in to haul me and other victims away to an unknown destination. My father and mother had come to see me off, just to make sure.

Chaps in uniform were piling into the train. I was saying farewell to my parents while trying to loosen Dad's grip on what I thought was his wallet. Now the carriages were packed. Somebody blew a whistle. With a final tug at the heartstrings and at Father's fingers, I darted across the platform, leapt into the nearest coach and clambered over the crowd into the only vacant space—the luggage rack.

Comfortably settled, with a warm glow of satisfaction, I began to examine my prize. I experienced a sinking feeling. What I had in my grasp wasn't Dad's wallet at all; it was only a magazine.

As I began to turn the pages, I settled gracefully on to the heads of the chaps in the seat below me. The sinking feeling stopped. I found myself engrossed in The Reader's Digest. It was a real pick-me-up. I forgot all about Dad's wallet. I went on reading all the way to Salisbury Plain.

Figuratively speaking, I have never stopped reading the Digest. Seriously, I have it every month, and in addition to the information and fun I get from the articles and features ("Picturesque Speech" is my favourite) I particularly enjoy the book condensations.

Nowadays, every time I see a luggage rack I remember the crime I perpetrated against my father. Yet I cannot feel regret, for it has let me into a life of so many enjoyments.

"BAGGY PANTS"

By William Brougher
Brigadier-General,
U.S. Army, Retired

IT WAS two o'clock on a June morning in 1944 when suddenly our prison barracks came ablaze with light. In an instant Japanese officers and guards were everywhere. It was a surprise inspection: we would have no opportunity to hide, destroy or otherwise dispose of anything that might be considered contraband or incriminating. As we groggily stood at attention they ransacked our belongings and took any papers or books they found.

BRIGADIER-GENERAL Brougher was captured by the Japanese at Bataan when the American forces surrendered on April 9, 1942. For the next three and a half years he was a prisoner in nine camps in four countries, among them the camp of this story, Shirakawa, in southern Formosa. Of the 70 Americans of his division captured with him, it is believed that only eight survive.

I was thoroughly alarmed. In the two years since my capture I had been scribbling down events, thoughts and feelings in a series of notebooks. I had even put together a little book of verse, harmless enough on the surface, but reflecting the grim experiences of prison life. To write had become an obsession with me, an absorbing interest, something to keep my hands busy, my mind occupied. In conditions of degradation and wretchedness it was my way of holding on to sanity.

It was a reckless pastime. General Jonathan Wainwright, who was a prisoner in the same camp, warned me of the risk I was taking in putting such things on paper. Our captors were extremely quick to resent anything we did or said that was uncomplimentary to them. And their resentment frequently took the form of violent reprisals. Naturally there was much in my pathetic scribblings that was considerably less than praise for the Japanese.

As I saw my notebooks carried off, I knew I was in for a rough time. From that moment on, I trembled every time I caught sight of the camp commandant or of his lieutenant, whom we called "Baggy Pants."

Baggy Pants was the incarnation of everything we despised about our barbed-wire existence — the bad food, filth, punishments, the very humiliation of having been captured in the first place. A big hulk of a man, he wore his pants bagged down over the tops of his boots, and had a kind of shuffling gait. He spoke English fairly well, and we suspected he was aware of our familiar reference to him.

It wasn't long before the Japanese began summoning the prisoners whose papers they had taken. Being extremely methodical, they started with men whose names began with A, then worked into the B's. A British brigadier whose papers turned up something our captors didn't like was thrown into solitary confinement on bread and water for three days. A U.S. Army colonel was terrifyingly beaten, then ordered to return each day for more of the same. It wouldn't be long before my name was reached.

To quieten my anxiety I spent as much time as possible in the post-age-stamp-size garden I had been allowed to cultivate inside the prison compound. Only 10 by 20 feet, that garden was now my only diversion—and a great source of pride. My 12 tomato plants were eight feet tall and heavy with ripe fruit. My white radishes, cabbage and kohlrabi might have taken prizes at an agricultural show.

I was hoeing round the roots of the tomato plants one afternoon when I heard a shuffle behind me. A voice asked crisply: "Your name is—*Blauer?*"

It was Baggy Pants! Like many Japanese he sometimes substituted *l* for *r* in speaking English, and I was sure it was me he was after. My turn for punishment had come!

I dropped my hoe, stiffened my arms at my side and bowed low in the approved manner. Baggy Pants had a large envelope in his hand, and his face was intensely serious. Before I could utter a word, he asked again: "Your name — Blauer?"

"Yes, I am Brougher," I answered.

"I have your books here," he said. "I lead."

He pulled one of my notebooks from the envelope, his expression still severe.

"You lite poetly?" he asked.

This was a puzzling start. "Well," I answered cautiously, "I try to write verse."

"How long you lite poetly?"

Here was something new in the way of booby traps. I realized vaguely that he was slipping up on my weak side. But I was already a little off guard.

"Well," I said, trying to appear casual, "I've worked at it off and on most of my life."

He opened the notebook and moved close to me.

"You lite some velly beautiful things. You gleat poet in Amelika?"

I searched for the note of sarcasm in his voice, the smirk of ridicule on his face. But he was completely serious.

"Oh no," I assured him. "I'm no poet. I'm a soldier. I merely fool around with verse. Did you really read my pieces?"

"Yes, yes, I lead all many times," replied Baggy Pants.

What was this leading to? I would open my mouth and put my foot in it for sure. But I could not hold back the eager question that every would-be poet must ask of one who has read his verse: "Did you —did you like any of my pieces?"

"Yes," said Baggy Pants. "Some pieces I like velly much. I no judge poetly, you know, but I like."

By this time I was peering over his shoulder at my notebook, forgetting that I was supposed to remain at attention.

"Which piece did you like?"

Baggy Pants' tough face actually smiled.

"I like best the one you lite about you wife. And this one you lite

about family. This one I have—how you say—memolize?"

He had the book open at a verse containing only 38 words. Without looking at the text he began to recite it. Its sentiment suffered little by being spoken in his peculiar English. But he faltered after a few lines and handed me the book.

"My English no good to lead poetly. You please lead it to me."

My defences were completely down. Here I was, a poet with an appreciative audience! Never was there a greater thrill than mine as I stood in my drab prison garb, flanked by tomato plants and cabbages and read my composition:

> When twilight falls and silence calls
> To evening prayer,
> Fair forms appear and hover near
> About my chair.
> Soft hands entwine themselves in mine,
> Lips touch my face;
> Then miles are not, and time's forgot,
> As souls embrace.

"That good! That good!" applauded Baggy Pants. "We feel same way too. I not see my family now long time. I like you piece."

"You like poetry?" I said.

"Oh yes, yes. We Japanese love poetly. The Emperor make it. All gleat Japanese make poems."

"Well, that's most interesting," I said. "Have you perhaps written some yourself?"

Baggy Pants fumbled and blushed

like a bashful, awkward schoolboy.

"Yes, I tly," he admitted hesitantly, scuffing the earth with the toe of his boot. "I tly, but I no good. I not make nice poetly like you. I study law, but no good poet."

All caution gone, I took the final fatal plunge. "Would you, perhaps, show me one of your verses?"

"You would lead my poem?" he asked with surprised and humble pleasure. "It no good—no good. But maybe you help. Maybe you help this tlanslation in English?"

He handed me a sheet of paper with a few lines typed on it. I read it aloud:

> The moon is high in the autumn
>   sky,
>   The light is like silver snow on
>   the grass,
> My body is weary with much
>   striving,
>   My soul is at peace.

My voice broke slightly as I spoke the last line.

"Why, Bag——" I caught myself just before uttering the hated nickname. He laughed.

"Baggy Pants! Yes, I know. Okay, okay, Baggy Pants, yes." He shrugged and looked down at his trousers. Then he looked at me.

"You like my poem?"

"It's beautiful," I said, and I meant it. "Don't change it."

"Thank you, thank you." He carefully folded the paper, put it back in his pocket, and handed me the envelope containing my confiscated scribblings.

"Your papers—General."

As he spoke my title, he made an instinctive motion as if to stiffen up and salute. Then he turned and started to walk away, but paused and came back.

"You have nice vegetables. We Japanese love beautiful garden. Beautiful garden; beautiful poetly. Would you — would you shake hand?"

I would. And I did.

〜〜〜〜〜〜〜

One Way to Give Up Smoking

An Army doctor has suggested a method for losing the tobacco habit which might work for some people. Each day the smoker postpones for one hour longer that first cigarette.

On the first day, as many cigarettes as desired may be smoked. On the second day, the first cigarette is put off for one hour, but after that the smoker consumes as many as he wishes. On the third day, no cigarettes are smoked until two hours after rising, but, again, as many thereafter as are craved. If the programme is carried out, smoking will cease in about two weeks. The theory is that if the smoker can consume an unlimited number of cigarettes after his period of abstinence, he loses his fear of the programme. —Peter Briggs in *Ladies' Home Journal*

"*Your Move, Hungarian!*"

By
Ferenc Laszlo

I was trying hard to swallow back my anxiety, that September morning in 1946, as I stood in the dismal Keleti railway station in Budapest. Panic, I knew, could wreck my hopes. I was waiting prayerfully for the name of Oscar Zinner to be called—even though I knew that this might mean my doom.

ÐÐÐÐÐÐÐÐÐÐÐÐÐÐ◁◁◁◁◁◁◁◁◁◁◁◁◁

The true identity of "Ferenc Laszlo" and certain details surrounding his escape from Hungary must, for obvious reasons, remain concealed. Under his right name he received special commendation from the highest Allied authorities for his intelligence activities. In the preparation of this article he had the assistance of David Savage, who has written extensively for radio and television.

Until ten days before, I had never heard of Oscar Zinner. Then an old friend of mine, who had information about the evacuation of Austrians living in Budapest, had come to see me in secret.

"One man on the list for resettlement," he said, "has not replied to letters informing him about the last train taking Austrian refugees home to Vienna. He may even be dead. This man is a portrait painter named Oscar Zinner. Would you care to risk attempting the trip to freedom under his name?"

Would I! It was imperative that I flee from my country as soon as possible. During the Nazi occupation, and later as an unwilling subject of

Hungary's Communist régime, I had been an Allied intelligence agent in Budapest. But recently the Soviet trap had snapped shut on several of my close colleagues. My usefulness to my country was at an end, and I had gone into hiding.

In changing my identity from Ferenc Laszlo to Oscar Zinner no passports would be involved, since the Russians had looted and burned all documents in virtually every Budapest home. My friend spread typewritten pages of Zinner's biographical data before me.

"You are now the painter, Oscar Zinner," he said. "Sit down and learn. You must become Zinner in every action, in every thought."

He tapped the papers. "The Communist frontier guards will have a copy of this. I need not tell you how closely they check. Another copy will be held by the supervisor of your group. He does not know Zinner. But when the name is called out at the station, *wait* before replying."

"Wait?" I asked.

"There's a chance that Zinner might turn up at the last minute," he explained. "If two of you should answer, it would be embarrassing for the one who wasn't Zinner."

For the next few days I studied Oscar Zinner's life story until I knew almost as much about him as I did about myself. I could describe the house where he was born in Graz. I knew his educational background, his habits, his likes and dislikes, even his style of painting. I could recall what critics had said of his pictures, the prices the paintings had brought and who had purchased them.

Finally, late the night before my scheduled departure, I crossed the Franz Josef Bridge and let the incriminating biographical notes, torn into shreds, flutter into the Danube.

A sudden crackle from the loudspeaker in the railway station snapped me back to the present. A rasping voice began to call out a list of names, alphabetically.

My stomach was knotted. Why did my new name have to begin with the last letter of the alphabet? I shoved my hands deep into my pockets to hide their trembling.

Finally, "Zinner—Oscar Zinner!" the voice barked.

I wanted to shout. But instead I waited, my heart pounding, my ears straining, my mind praying that there would be no answer.

"Zinner!" the voice called again, this time with annoyance.

I stepped forward. "Here!" I said timidly.

There was no challenge from the real Zinner. So far, all was well. We were separated into groups of ten and herded into compartments on the train.

Over and over again I unrolled the story in my head. "I am a portrait painter. I was born in Graz. My father was an architect. . . ."

A shrill whistle from the station platform signalled the train to start. It didn't move. Suddenly, voices speaking in Russian could be heard at the end of our coach. Four Soviet officers marched past our compartment door. They stopped at the next compartment, and I heard them order the occupants out into the corridor. Then they took over the space and soon they were laughing and shouting amid much clinking of glasses. The whistle blew again and the train jerked into movement.

As we picked up speed, I wondered when I should see my country again. But I realized suddenly that sadness was out of place. I was now Oscar Zinner, going home to Vienna.

The train groaned to a halt at Kelenföld. This was check-point number one. We did not have to wait long for the Soviet inspecting officer and his interpreter. In the corridor, accompanying Russian soldiers, heavily armed, stood stolidly watching.

The Soviet officer, a rock-faced little man, started with the woman opposite. Shuffling the flimsy biographical sheets, he barked questions in Russian which the interpreter translated into German. He came to the man sitting next to the window on my side of the compartment. I began rehearsing once again what I would say: "I am a painter. I was born in Graz. My name is . . . My name is . . ."

Sweat leapt out on my forehead, and my heart slid into my throat. A strange mental block, caused doubtless by my nervous tension and suppressed panic, let me remember everything about the man I was pretending to be except his name!

From a misty distance I heard the sharp voices of the examiner and the interpreter as they moved towards the woman beside me.

"Please, God," I prayed, "what is my name? I am a portrait painter. I was born in Graz. My name is . . ." It was no use. The name would not come.

Just then I heard the door of the next compartment slide open. There was a brief flurry of conversation in the corridor, and then a Red Army colonel poked his head into our compartment.

"Wer spielt Schach?" he asked gruffly in bad German. "Who plays chess?"

Our examining officer turned and glared at the interruption, then stepped back respectfully under the gaze of his superior. As I was closest to the door the colonel's next question was directed at me.

"Spielen Sie Schach?" he asked.

I hadn't played chess for ten years, but it didn't matter. This was the breathing spell I needed. No one else in the compartment spoke.

"Ja. Ich spiele Schach," I said.

The colonel gestured to me to follow him.

In the Russians' compartment were two other colonels and one much-bemedalled general, a fattening but still powerful giant in his early 50's. Evidently it was he who wanted a game, for he muttered a curt acknowledgment to the officer who brought me, and gestured me to a seat opposite him.

Beside me were dozens of sandwiches and a box of sweets. On the small table under the window were glasses, vodka, Hungarian brandy and wine. The general gave me an appraising look, then pointed to the food and vodka. *"Davai,"* he growled in Russian. "Go on."

I ate in tortured suspense. At any moment one of the Russians might ask my name; or worse, the examiner might intrude.

As the train started, the general produced a chessboard and began arranging the men.

"God help me," I thought. "This is the game of my life. I must make it good, and yet I can't afford to win." I had never known a Russian who didn't hate to lose. And I had never known a chess player who liked to play for long unless his opponent could make it interesting.

As we played, some of the tricks of the game slowly returned to me. The other officers watched the game in deferential silence, apparently believing that the general was a wizard at it. As a matter of fact he was quite a good player, but I was able to make him work for every advantage.

Time flew, as it does on every tense battlefield of chess, and with a start I realized that the train was slowing down at Győr, our checkpoint number two. Once again my mind began to race. Now the door of the compartment slid open, and the supervisor of the Austrian group stepped in. "This man has not yet been questioned," he said firmly.

I need not have worried. Without a word the general rose, spread his huge bear's paw of a hand against the man's chest and expelled him into the corridor. Then he slammed the door and pointed to the chessboard.

"Davai, Magyar!" he thundered. "Your move, Hungarian!"

Hungarian! I *was* coming from Hungary, of course, but his slip of the tongue, if it was that, set my scalp tingling. Once or twice after that I thought I caught him looking at me strangely, but each time he returned his gaze to the board.

When we finished the first game, from which the general emerged the victor, he said something to the officer who spoke German. "The general enjoys your style," the latter interpreted. "He will play another game."

Before we began again, however, the general insisted that we drink. Reckless with the warm flood of confidence that came from the vodka, I lost myself in this game and suddenly found myself on the brink of winning. We were in the last crucial moves as the train slowed for Hegyeshalom, our final check-point. Here I would win or lose—not merely a game but everything I lived for.

This time dozens of Red soldiers, rifles slung over their shoulders, grenades hanging from their belts, led the procession of interpreters and security guards. They merely glanced into our compartment and went on to the next. There the angry little group leader must have told them of the "Austrian" who was sitting with the officers, for one guard came back to investigate. He stepped smartly in at the door, saluted and spoke rapidly in Russian, at the same time pointing at me.

Once again my brain froze in fear. Surely the general would let them question me, if only to forestall any further interruptions. "I am a portrait painter and my name is . . ." I began saying to myself desperately. But I could not remember.

As the guard spoke, the general's face slowly turned purple. I had no idea what the guard was telling him, but it made him as angry as any man I'd ever seen. He looked at me, his eyes blazing. Then he carefully placed the chessboard on the table under the window and stood up.

"This is the end for me," I thought. "To come so close——"

The general crossed his arm in front of his body as a man would to draw a sword. When he brought it up in a sweeping arc, the back of his hand smashed across the guard's mouth. The man reeled backwards and struck the corridor wall.

The general slammed the door so hard that it shook our window, then returned to his seat, muttering something under his breath. He picked up the chessboard and studied the pieces.

"Davai, Magyar!" he said.

My heart was bursting with relief. No one would dare come in again— of that I was sure. As the train gathered speed, release from the awful tension flooded over me so that, for the first time, I smiled. The general looked up from his study of the board and smiled in return. He spoke to the young officer, who said to me, "The general wonders if you would enjoy playing him again some time in Vienna. Where can he reach you?"

Automatically I mentioned a well-known Vienna hotel. "And your name?" prodded the young officer.

Now, without the awful, clutching terror, I hesitated but a moment. How could I ever have forgotten those two simple words, I wondered.

Aloud I said, "My name is Oscar Zinner."

Reports to the Home Front. Youngster writing home from boarding school: "Send food parcels! All they serve here is breakfast, lunch and supper" (*The Diners' Club News*) . . . A father received a birthday parcel from his son away at school. Inside was a set of inexpensive cuff links and a matching tie-pin with this note: "Dear Father: This isn't much, but it's all you can afford" (AP)

Humour in Uniform

DURING THE fuel oil emergency caused by the Suez Canal closure, we were running a tanker with little leave or liberty. One evening an officer remarked, "This duty really separates the men from the boys."

"Worse still," another officer spoke up, "it separates the boys from the girls!"
—LIEUTENANT-COMMANDER W. J. CLARE

A PARTICULARLY scruffy private in my platoon was always being picked on by the sergeant because of the state of his uniform. Gazing at him in disgust one morning, the sergeant exclaimed, "Smith, I don't mind your not cleaning your cap-badge, really I don't, but *please* weed it now and again!"
—FRANK ELLIS

TWO DOORS away from us when we lived at an overseas base was a most attractive young wife, who frequently appeared in her garden dressed in very short shorts and a halter. Coming out of my quarters one day, I noticed that she was working in her garden in her usual attire. While getting an eyeful, I opened my car door and got in to drive to my office. Reaching for the starter, I discovered, much to my dismay—and to the amusement of my wife, who happened to be looking out of the window—that I was sitting in the back seat.
—A. T. LEARNARD

IN A shop ashore a petty officer was consulting a friend about what size sweater to buy for his girl. After much discussion, the friend finally said, "Oh well, you can't go wrong. If it's too big, she'll be flattered, and if it's too small, she'll wear it!"
—H. H. HUGGINS

MY BROTHER, a general's aide-de-camp, was making arrangements for an officers' party to be held in an Italian yacht club. The windows, which were port-holes, had to be blacked out, since it was wartime. My brother took wooden discs to a soldier who was good at drawing and asked him to decorate them and deliver them to the club in time for the party.

The party wasn't as lively as it might have been. Every time a beribboned staff officer lifted his eyes, he found himself staring into the stubbly face of a dirty, weary, disapproving soldier peering through the port-hole.
—J. C. KING

WHILE STATIONED in North Africa, our unit was harassed by a hard-nosed, obnoxious sergeant-major, who believed that every efficient sergeant had to be tough. He drove us unmercifully, often saying, "Some day you riff-raff will appreciate me."

At last he received transfer orders, and a "going-away party for the sarge" was scheduled. The sarge was overjoyed that at last he had found a bunch of men who appreciated him. His joy faded when he realized that his date of departure was the day *before* the party.
—J. EASON

The
Reader's Digest

VOLUME 73

AUGUST 1958

© 1958 by The Reader's Digest Association Ltd.

*The "impossible" experience
of an RAF rear-gunner, grippingly told in
a Reader's Digest "First Person" Award Story*

"I FELL 18,000 FEET WITHOUT A PARACHUTE"

By Nicholas Stephen Alkemade
ex-Warrant Officer, Royal Air Force

AT 21,000 feet the rear turret of a Lancaster bomber is a cold and lonely place, separated from the rest of the crew by two sets of doors and 12 yards of fuselage. It's a cramped space, little more than a shell for the body of the gunner, clad in his bulky flying clothes. There is not even room for him to wear a parachute—only the harness; his chute pack is stowed in the main fuselage, a few feet inside the second door, and separate from the other crew members' packs.

In an emergency the gunner has to leave his turret, get his chute pack, hook it on to the harness, then bale out, hoping that the trailing radio aerial will not cut him in two. Being a "Tail-End Charlie" was rated by the RAF a "hazardous occupation."

NICHOLAS ALKEMADE, son of a Dutch father and English mother, was born in North Walsham, Norfolk. He joined the RAF in 1940 at 18 and served in Air-Sea Rescue launches until, "wanting more excitement," he transferred to Bomber Command as a rear-gunner.

As our Lancaster neared Berlin on the night of March 24–25, 1944, we could see the long fingers of searchlight beams probing the sky. Closing in, we spotted the sparkling red and green markers laid down for us by our Pathfinders ahead. Plane after plane made its bombing run, and fireworks erupted below us: golden incendiary fires, brilliant white and red explosions and the orange flashes of ack-ack guns. Then . . .

Bombs away! Our own 4,000-pound "cookie" and three tons of incendiaries hurtled downwards. Through weaving searchlight beams we turned for home, keeping a sharp watch for Jerry night fighters. I could see them at work in the distance. A flash of white light would burst into a great red-and-orange ball of fire, to arc across the sky towards the black earth below. Some poor "Lanc" had got it, and some of my chums would not return to base.

We were somewhere over the Ruhr when suddenly a series of shuddering crashes raked our aircraft from nose to tail, then two terrific thunderclaps as two cannon shells exploded on my turret ring mounting. The plexiglass blister shattered and vanished—one large fragment slicing into my right leg.

Luckily my turret had been facing astern. I quickly depressed my guns and stared out. Not more than 50 yards from me was the shadowy outline of a Junkers 88 fighter, his leading edge a line of brilliant white flashes as he blazed away at our wounded ship. I aimed point-blank and squeezed the trigger of my four banked 303 Brownings. They fired simultaneously and the Junkers was transfixed by four streams of fiery tracers. He peeled off, his port engine trailing flame. I did not watch to see his fate; I was too concerned about my own.

Flaming fuel from our tanks was streaking past me. On the intercom I started to report to the captain that the tail was on fire, but he cut me short with, "I can't hold her for long, lads. You'll have to jump. Bale out! Bale out!"

Flicking the turret doors behind me open with my elbows, I turned and opened the fuselage door beyond—and stared for a horrified instant into a giant cauldron. Flame and smoke swept towards me. I recoiled, choking and blinded, into my turret. But I *had to get my chute!* I opened the doors again and lunged for the pack.

Too late! The case had been burnt off and the tightly-packed silk was springing out, fold after fold, and vanishing in puffs of flame.

In the turret I took stock. Here I was, only 21 years old, and this was the end of the road. Already oil from the turret's hydraulic system was on fire and flames seared my face and hands. At any moment the doomed aircraft might explode.

Should I endure this roasting hell or should I jump? If I was to die, better a quick, painless end by diving into the ground . . . Quickly I hand-rotated my turret abeam, flipped the doors open and, in an agony of despair, somersaulted backwards into the night.

OH, THE blessed relief of being away from that shrivelling heat! Gratefully I felt the cold air against my face. I had no sensation of falling. It was more like being at rest on an airy cloud. Looking down I saw the stars beneath my feet.

"Must be falling head first," I thought.

If this was dying it was nothing to be afraid of. I only regretted that I should go without saying good-bye to my friends. I would never again see Pearl, my sweetheart back home in Loughborough. And I'd been due to go on leave the following Sunday.

Then—nothing. I must have blacked out.

IN SLOW stages my senses returned. First there was an awareness of light above me which gradually became a patch of starlit sky. The light was framed in an irregular opening that finally materialized as a hole in thickly interlaced boughs of fir trees. I seemed to be lying in a deep mound of underbrush heavily blanketed with snow.

It was bitterly cold. My head throbbed and there was terrible pain in my back. I felt all over my body. I found I could move my legs. I was all in one piece. In a sudden up-welling of unworthiness and of delight,

A BODY falling freely in space, with no resistance of air, would drop 16 feet the first second, 48 feet during the next, 80 feet in the third, etc. Falling from 18,000 feet, therefore, it would attain a final speed of 730 miles per hour before crashing to the earth.

A body falling through the atmosphere, however, is retarded by the resistance of the air. Because of this, Sergeant Alkemade's "terminal" speed has been estimated at approximately 122 miles per hour. His incredible survival can be attributed only to the fact that the final stage of his fall was cushioned, first by the thickly interlaced branches of fir trees, and further by the heavy, snow-covered brush on which he landed.

the very first thought to flash into my conscious mind was a heartfelt prayer of thanksgiving, of humble praise and utter wonderment. On the floor of the little patch of fir forest, into which I had hurtled parachuteless from a hell three and two-fifths miles above it, this was not blasphemy. "Jesus Christ," I said. "I'm alive!"

I tried to sit up—but it hurt too much. Craning my neck I could see that my flying boots were gone and my clothes scorched and tattered. I began to be afraid of freezing to death. In the pocket of my tunic I found the flat tin, badly bent, in which I kept my cigarettes and my lighter. The cigarettes were unharmed; I lit up. My watch, I found, was still ticking. The luminous hands showed 3.20; it had been close to midnight when our aircraft was hit.

Attached to my collar was the whistle for use in case of ditching at sea to keep crew members in contact with one another.

"Here is one man who is happy to become a prisoner of war," I said to myself. From time to time I blew the whistle. It seemed hours later I heard a far-off "Hulloo!"

I kept whistling and the answering shouts grew closer. At last I could see flashlights approaching. Then some men and boys were standing over me. After relieving me of my cigarettes they growled, "'raus! Heraus!" ("Get up!") When they saw I couldn't they put a tarpaulin under me and dragged me across a frozen pasture to a cottage. There an old lady with a gnarled but kindly face gave me the finest egg nog I ever tasted.

As I lay on the floor I heard a car pull up outside. Two men in plain clothes clumped into the room. They looked me over carefully. Then, quite indifferent to my pain, they yanked me to my feet and bundled me out to their car. We seemed to hit all the bumps on our way to a hospital.

I was a long time in the operating room. Only later did I learn the sum of my injuries: burnt legs, twisted right knee, a deep splinter wound in my thigh, strained back, slight concussion and a deep scalp wound; first-, second- and third-degree burns on face and hands. Most of this damage I had sustained before jumping.

Finally, cleaned up and with most of the plexiglass fragments picked out of me, I was installed in a clean bed—but not to sleep! In came a tall, pompous character in a *Wehrmacht* uniform, thin as a hatchet in the face and wearing rimless glasses. Through an interpreter, a young convalescent soldier, he asked me the usual, probing questions: What targets did you attack? Where is your base? How many aircraft are there at your base? . . . and many others. I stated my name, rank and number. To the other questions I could only reply, "I am not allowed to answer."

Then they began asking about my parachute. "Where did you hide it? Did you bury it?" (Spies dropping into enemy territory commonly concealed their parachutes; airmen falling out of sky battles did not.)

"Parachute?" I said. "I didn't use one!"

I thought Hatchet-Face would burst with rage. He let out a stream of oaths, then turned on his heel and stalked out. For three days the questioning was repeated. Finally I was left alone.

After three weeks, when my wounds were fairly healed, I was whisked off to Dulag Luft near Frankfurt and put into solitary confinement. The time gave me opportunity to think out how I might convince my interrogators that my incredible story was true.

So I was ready when a week later a young *Luftwaffe* lieutenant led me into the office of the *Kommandant* of Dulag Luft. On the *Kommandant's* desk I was amused to see a packet of English cigarettes and a bar of chocolate.

"We have to congratulate you, I understand, Sergeant," the *Kommandant* said drily, in excellent English. "Would you tell me all about your remarkable escape yourself, please? I have only a garbled account from the *Herr Leutnant*. I gather you claim to have jumped from a blazing bomber at a height of 6,000 metres without a parachute —a very tall story, Sergeant, *nicht wahr?*"

He could prove the story if he cared to, I told him. Hadn't a wrecked Lancaster fallen in the area on the night of March 24–25? If so, that would be the plane I had jumped from. The burnt remnants of my parachute pack could be found just forward of the rear fuselage door. Also, he could examine my parachute harness—to see for himself that *it had never been used*.

The *Kommandant* listened to me in silence. "A really remarkable story," he said—"and I hear many!"

He fired some rapid German at the lieutenant, who saluted and left.

The *Kommandant* handed me a cigarette and we chatted pleasantly for the next quarter of an hour. Then the lieutenant, waving my parachute harness, burst into the office with three other officers, all shouting excitedly in German.

The lieutenant flung the harness on to the desk, pointed to the snap-hooks that were still in their clips and the lift webs still fastened down on the chest straps. The *Kommandant* soberly took in these facts, then leant back in his chair and studied each of us thoughtfully in turn. I'll never forget his next words; he spoke in English:

"Gentlemen! A miracle—no less!"

He rose, came round his desk and offered me his hand. I took it. "Congratulations, my boy, on being alive! What a story to tell your grandchildren!"

Then I was assailed with slaps on the back, handshaking and vociferous good wishes. The *Kommandant* dismissed me with, "Tomorrow, I promise, your comrades will be told about how you became a POW."

In the *Kommandant's* office next morning I saw that the *Luftwaffe* authorities had been busy. On his desk lay some pieces of scorched metal, including the D-handle of a parachute ripcord and a piece of wire that would be the ripcord itself.

"The remains of your parachute pack," the *Kommandant* explained. "We found it where you said it

would be. To us it is the final proof."

The wrecked Lancaster lay about 20 kilometres from where I had landed, I was told. Four crew members had been burnt to death and had been buried in a military cemetery near Meschede with full military honours. From their names and numbers I realized that only "Ginger" Cleary, our navigator, Geoff Burwell, the radio operator, and myself were left. (They had been blown clear in the final explosion, I learnt later.)

A German flying-officer and two NCO's marched me into the compound, where some 200 captured Allied flyers were assembled. I was directed to stand on a bench. Then the *Luftwaffe* officer recounted my story to the incredulous airmen.

There was pandemonium. Nationalities were forgotten. I was mobbed by French, German, British and Yank, shaking my hand, shouting questions, forcing upon me gifts of a cigarette or a square of chocolate. Then I was presented with a paper, signed by the senior British officer at the demonstration, who had taken down the German authentication in writing and had it witnessed by the two senior British NCO's. It is only a faded scrap of paper but it will always be the proudest thing I own:

Dulag Luft
"It has been investigated and corroborated by the German authorities that the claim made by

Sgt. Alkemade, 1431537 RAF, is true in all respects, namely, that he made a descent from 18,000 feet without a parachute and made a safe landing without injury, his parachute having been on fire in the aircraft. He landed in deep snow among fir trees.

Corroboration witnessed by
F/Lt. H. J. Moore
Senior British Officer
F/Sgt. R. R. Lamb 1339582
F/Sgt. T. A. Jones 411
Senior British NCO's
Date: 25/4/44

After liberation came in May 1945, RAF Intelligence checked the records at Dulag Luft, found the reports of my strange adventure to be true and included them in the official records of the Royal Air Force.

Today Pearl and I are living happily in Loughborough, where I am a buyer in a department store. (Geoff Burwell was best man at our wedding.) I have taken the first important steps towards following the *Kommandant's* advice—to tell my story to my grandchildren. I'll have to wait, though, till little Valerie and Nicholas provide me with grandchildren to hear it.

In the meantime, I can only wonder why such a marvellous thing should have happened to a man as ordinary as myself.

Poles Apart

A FAVOURITE story at Macy's Department Store in New York, and a true one, is about the customer who ordered a flagpole to be delivered in time for a national holiday. His letter specified the required dimensions and the flagpole was forthwith delivered, but when he had installed it on the lawn it turned out to be too short. After a spirited telephone message from the customer, Macy's rushed a lorry to deliver a second flagpole and take the first one away. Alas! The second flagpole, laboriously embedded, proved to be too long.

Disgusted, the patriotic customer dug it up and threw it behind the garage. Then he went into the village, bought a local flagpole to his liking and planted it on the lawn with great sweating. Exhausted, he tottered into his house, called up Macy's and gave them a piece of his mind; they could take back their lousy flagpole, he told them, and never mind sending another one either.

The next day was the day before the holiday. In the householder's absence, a lorry drove up, two men descended and, with a mighty effort, uprooted the flagpole from the lawn and carted it back to Macy's.

"We were sent to pick up a flagpole, and that was the only flagpole we *saw!*" they declared later.
—M. C. H.

The Man Who Flew Wingate's Gliders

Portrait of one of the legendary figures of the Second World War

By John Alison

W<small>E WERE</small> both air cadets when we met in 1936. He was short, square-jawed, smiling, his thick wavy hair already prematurely grey. His name was Phil Cochran and he looked anything but what he was: a former choirboy. He had instinctive strut and dash, and you felt in him immediately the qualities of leadership that were to make him one of the legendary figures of the Second World War.

Phil was only 26 then, and just learning to fly, but his rich vocabulary, his irreverence and general savvy caused the rest of us cadets to look upon him as the Old Man.

I was immediately attracted to this rollicking, picturesque Irishman, who loved jazz, pretty girls and, above all, flying. He was the perfect embodiment of the hot pilot.

As we moved along in our training Phil worked ceaselessly to perfect himself and the squadron he came to command. He loved to experiment, to try the unorthodox. By now I had a squadron, too, and we'd have mock air battles all the morning and refight the battles at lunch while the food got cold.

After the outbreak of war I was posted to the Far East with General Claire Chennault's Flying Tigers. Phil went to North Africa. Under his inspired leadership his inexperienced squadron fought a wild guerrilla war over 20,000 square miles of southern Tunisia.

Phil turned his fighter planes into fighter-bombers by strapping bombs to them and used the technique of skip-bombing. Once he strapped a bomb to his plane and dropped it on a German general's headquarters at Kairouan, flying in so low he had to zoom up to get over the one-storey building.

Living in a dug-out, scrounging for supplies, flying so incessantly that he barely had time to eat and sleep, Cochran became a legend among his men. "He dominated his world from Tebessa onwards," wrote Vincent Sheean. "He seemed a kind of electrical disturbance in human form, and he infected the very ground with the delusion that it belonged to him."

When North Africa fell to the Allies, Cochran returned to the United States and soon was summoned to Washington. The Allied leaders had agreed on a plan to retake Burma by invasion from India. Britain was to furnish the ground forces under General Orde Wingate, the dour, mystical Scotsman whom Churchill called "another Lawrence of Arabia." America would furnish the air support, led by Phil, with me as his deputy commander. We were to support Wingate with light planes, supplying his forces and evacuating the wounded.

"But we're *fighter* pilots!" Phil flared when General "Hap" Arnold outlined the assignment.

General Arnold continued explaining the plan, with a twinkle in his eye. We gathered that although we were to support the land drive, he wouldn't mind if we turned it into an air show. That twinkle was all Phil needed. But how could you make an air show out of flying support for men and mules trudging slowly through the jungle? Then inspiration struck—gliders! Why not leap the troops *over* the jungle to land behind enemy lines?

Arnold, who called Phil "the toughest little Irishman I've ever seen," told him to draw up a list of what he needed. Then we set out scrounging — dog-trotting through the corridors of the Pentagon, pounding on doors to beg, borrow or steal the men and equipment. We got 500 men, pilots and glider specialists; 30 rocket-firing P-51 Mustangs; transport planes; a squadron of Mitchell bombers, 150 light planes and 150 gliders. Our glider pilots trained in North Carolina.

"People who fly planes are fool enough," Phil said, as we watched the big, lumbering craft, "but anyone who gets into one of those things is a damn fool." Then, after a few minutes: "Well, let's find out how to fly one of these contraptions ourselves."

After learning to fly a glider, Phil tried snatching gliders off the ground with speeding planes—a new and ticklish technique. He kept working at it, riding in a snatched-up glider himself, until our pilots had perfected the perilous manoeuvre.

With our Air Commandos finally trained, Phil flew to Delhi to join Wingate. He arrived to find the campaign cancelled; scrubbed, Wingate said bitterly, for lack of air transport. Phil stormed that only a limited amount of transport would be needed since, in addition to the light planes Wingate was counting on, we had 150 gliders to haul supplies. Wingate's dark eyes widened as Phil explained that the gliders could also move a sizeable force of

Colonel Philip Cochran

troops. The general immediately spread a map on the floor and planned how his Chindits, airlifted deep into the jungle, could fan out from there and fight the Japanese.

Phil went before the South-east Asia Command. Round a table sat Lord Louis Mountbatten and Generals Auchinleck, Stilwell, Chennault and Stratemeyer. Phil's quick thinking and colourful vocabulary now stood him in good stead as he argued for his glider plan.

"My boy," Lord Mountbatten said finally, "you are the only ray of sunshine we've had in this theatre this year." The Burma invasion plan was reinstated.

When I landed in India Phil met me, bubbling with enthusiasm. We worked hard at our base in the Assam hill country, getting ready for the big push. We lived in grass huts in the jungle; there were tigers and pythons about, and baboons sometimes ran across the airfield. Morale was high among the men, although discipline, as usual under Phil, was lax.

Once Mountbatten came to our field and addressed the men. A

returning pilot, seeing the crowd gathered round a speaker on a jeep, assumed it was Cochran. Putting his Mustang into a dive he swept down at 500 m.p.h.—and buzzed Mountbatten's head. The tall Supreme Commander of the South-east Asia Theatre stood there without flinching, but Phil almost fainted. "That damn fool is new here, Lord Louis," he explained hastily. "He thought it was just me."

In preparation for the invasion, our planes began pounding Japanese bases in Burma. Although Phil, now 34, was old for a fighter pilot, he was in the thick of action. On one mission his plane was shot up and he was mistakenly reported killed. That time his local newspaper printed his obituary.

The all-airborne invasion of northern Burma was made on the night of March 5, 1944. Our transports took off after sundown, each plane towing two gliders jammed with troops and mules.

I piloted one of the leading gliders; Wingate had ordered Phil to stay back at headquarters with him. Our target was a jungle clearing (we called it "Broadway") 165 miles behind the Japanese lines in Burma.

It was almost a disaster. On the way, 17 gliders were lost—many of them over enemy territory. Of the gliders that landed, most piled up in buffalo wallows or in furrows hidden by the tall grass, where elephants had dragged teak logs. We would be frantically dragging wounded men and bucking mules out of one wrecked glider when we'd hear another whistling down through the darkness to smash into it. Finally we got our damaged radio working and, after 46 gliders had landed, stopped the rest from coming down.

Fortunately, our invasion caught the enemy by surprise and there was no immediate opposition. Soon we had a makeshift runway ready to receive more planes and gliders. The next night we occupied a second clearing, and then a third.

We built airstrips in the clearings, and from these new bases Phil and I and our fighter pilots harassed the Japanese. Phil used a trick he had developed in North Africa of equipping his plane with a weight on the end of a cable, zooming in low over Japanese telephone wires and ripping them out with the dangling cable.

In one month alone our fighters destroyed one-fifth of the Japanese air force in Burma, at one time destroying 100 planes on the ground in two days.

Then one day Wingate took off on an aerial inspection of our bases and his plane crashed in the jungle. Wingate, the dedicated, gaunt jungle general, was killed. After his death, and with the coming of the monsoon season, the campaign came to an end.

But Phil's Air Commandos and Wingate's Chindits had strangled

Japanese supply lines, contributing materially to the fall of northern Burma to Stilwell's army shortly afterwards.

IT ALL seems far away now. The Burma jungle has grown up again over the rutted old clearing called Broadway. The planes Phil Cochran flew seem as obsolete as armoured war horses, but his own qualities of daring and imagination and humour are vivid in my memory. Whenever I think of those adventurous days I see him on the dusty jungle runway, grey hair blowing in the slipstream, surrounded by his "kids," the fighter pilots and ground crews who worshipped him.

After the war Phil worked for more than a year in Hollywood, and directed the magnificent air-combat scenes in the film *Jet Pilot*.

The last time I saw him was a few months ago, in a quiet little church. He was holding a baby boy in his arms, smiling down at him—godfather at my son's christening.

Mistaken For Granted

AN OXFORD don had been asked to a children's party. Entering the house, he dropped down on all fours and crawled into the drawing-room growling like a bear. But the children's party was next door. He had blundered into a house where some astonished ladies were having tea. Too embarrassed to explain, he rose and fled without a word. The undignified don was the Rev. Charles Dodgson, better known as Lewis Carroll, author of *Alice in Wonderland*.

THE LINER *Queen Mary*, launched in 1934, got her name in an unexpected way. By tradition, Cunard ships were given names ending in "ia," and the company had decided to call the new liner *Queen Victoria*. The Cunard chairman went to see King George V and began telling him that they wanted to name the ship after one of England's most noble queens... "Oh," said the King before he could finish. "Her Majesty will be so pleased." So the liner became *Queen Mary*, and the King never knew that it was he who had given her the name.

HUMOUR
IN UNIFORM

AFTER MONTHS of ocean, ice and penguins, sailors of the Antarctic expedition were enjoying their first day of leave in Auckland, New Zealand. In a department store, I saw one of the sailors standing in front of me. He was gazing intently at the attractive blonde salesgirl. As she came to serve him, he waved her away. "Just looking, thanks!" he said as he continued to gaze at her admiringly. —JUDITH JONES

SCHEDULED TO do a show at an army hospital, comedian George Jessel decided to send a spray of flowers for each nurse. The flowers made a hit, for when Jessel appeared he observed that every nurse was wearing the floral offering.

There'd been just one oversight—all the nurses were male. —E. E. EDGAR

DURING OFFICE coffee breaks an attractive young married woman was always surrounded by admiring males, a situation entirely to her liking. But despite all her efforts, the office's most handsome bachelor remained oblivious of her charms. Attempting to attract his attention one morning she asked coyly, "What is the first thing you notice about a girl, Major Davis?"

"The third finger of her left hand," he replied curtly. —JEFF HOLLOWAY

AN OLD-GUARD sergeant in my husband's unit preferred to invest his money in a good game of cards rather than savings certificates. One day his section officer, intending to ridicule him, asked him to rise in the mess hall and explain why he refused to buy savings certificates.

"Well, sir," he said, "let's put it this way. I refuse to finance my own misery!" He sat down amid a roar of friendly laughter. —MRS. R. SCHAT

OUR PLANE, flying at about 16,000 feet, suddenly began to descend rapidly. A soldier sitting next to me turned and said: "I beg your pardon —does the ringing in my ears annoy you?" —LARRY ADLER in *Variety*

WHILE SERVING with a small infantry unit, I overheard a new recruit just out of training address the adjutant, a captain, as major. I called him aside and pointed out that three pips was the insignia of a captain, not a major.

"Look, sergeant," he said. "You got your stripes the way you wanted to. Now let me get mine my way!"

—L. E. MARTIN

TRAPPED!

The water rose to his knees,
his waist, his armpits—
a young sailor's terrible 20
hours in a sinking ship

By Lee Karsian
as told to Albert Rosenfeld

It was D-Day in the Philippines
—October 20, 1944. Troops were
already three miles inland on the
island of Leyte when, shortly after
4 p.m., a Japanese plane emerged
from the mists and loosed a torpedo
at the American cruiser Honolulu.
The explosion tore a jagged 25-foot
hole in the ship's port side, killing
60 men.

As the ship sagged over, the sea
flooded the third deck and part of
the second. But down on the third
deck there remained one isolated

pocket of air: the compartment known as Radio 3. And trapped inside Radio 3 was Lee Karsian, a 19-year-old radio operator.

At about noon, hot and tired, I had wandered into Radio 3, our emergency radio room. It was small, about 8 by 12 feet, but the fan in there felt wonderful. I closed the hatch, spread out a blanket, took off my shoes and went contentedly to sleep.

When I awoke, my watch said 4.05—already five minutes late for duty. I scrambled to my feet and bent down to get my shoes. Before I could straighten up again I felt myself weirdly lifted, then slammed face down on to the steel deck. In the same instant the lights went out, there was a lightning-quick flash of flame and a slow-building explosive roar. Things landed heavily on my back, a thick dust filled the air. I heard water rushing against the hatch, blood-freezing screams from outside—and then I blacked out.

I have no idea how much time passed before I came to. Smoke and dust filled my nostrils, and there was a foul taste in my mouth. I ached all over. The floor was wet under me. With great effort, I slid two metal transmitter plates off my back. Then in the darkness I staggered round the tilted deck.

Things looked bad. Water was coming in fast. The radio was dead. So was the battery on the emergency light. I took a heavy file from the workbench and banged on the bulkheads. No response. Sloshing round in the watery dark, I found a saucer-sized shrapnel hole, with water pouring in. I knew I was trapped, but I felt better after I had stuffed the hole with the innards of a mattress I found under the workbench. When I found a torch that worked, I felt even better—but not for long. The roving light revealed thousands of tiny holes the size of pinheads, through which oily water was seeping steadily. I began to feel panic.

Seized with a violent coughing fit, I leant weakly against the workbench for support. My torch went out, plunging me into blackness again. Now panic took a firmer grip. I felt like crying, I *wanted* to cry—but I couldn't.

Suddenly I remembered the phones that connected with the ship's intercom system. I waded over and frantically plugged them in, holding the earphones to my ears.

". . . Signals Aft testing with Signal Bridge." It was a familiar voice.

"John!" I said, surprised at the steadiness of my voice. "John, this is Lee Karsian."

"Lee Karsian? You're dead!" Then, "Where are you?"

"I'm trapped in Radio 3."

Everyone began cutting in on the line. A voice came in from the main deck. "This is Captain Thurber. Can you hear me? We'll do everything in our power to get you out as soon as possible. Then I heard Bill Gallagher, my closest friend. "Bill," I said, "I want the truth. Are we sinking?"

He hesitated. "Lee, they're lightening ship, trying to keep her afloat if they possibly can. If there's anything more, I'll let you know. I won't leave these phones for a minute."

Another coughing fit caught me in the pit of my stomach, and I passed out. But as my face hit the water, which was now over my knees, the shock revived me. I leant shakily against the bulkhead and lost all track of time.

Suddenly, "Karsian, can you hear me?" It was one of our officers.

"I'm sorry to have to tell you this, but it looks as if we're going to abandon ship. It's not official yet, but as soon as it is, one of our destroyers will be given the order to sink the ship. We'll ask them to make the hit as direct as possible."

The voice cut out, and Bill came back on. "Lee! Do you have anything you could knock yourself out with?"

I had already checked. The medicine kit contained a strip of easy-to-inject morphine capsules. "If I go down," I said, "I'll go down sleeping."

"Okay. I'll be the last guy off. When I go, you'll know it's time to use it." We both seemed terribly businesslike.

The next voice was Chaplain Sharkey's. The day before I had told him, jokingly, that I had tickets for a big football match. "I suppose I won't get to use those tickets after all," I said feebly.

"No, I suppose not," the chaplain said.

I passed out again, then gradually became aware of the chaplain's voice: ". . . walk through the valley of the shadow of death, I will fear no evil, for Thou art with me. Thy rod and Thy staff, they comfort me . . ." I did feel comforted. Then, with a sickening jolt, I realized what the chaplain was doing. *He was reading my funeral service!*

His voice droned on, but my mind strayed. I thought of my home. I could see my father listening to the radio, my mother finishing the washing-up in the kitchen. Suddenly the chaplain's voice stopped.

"Bill!" I called in panic. "Bill!"

"Yes, Lee. Listen—it looks as if we have a reprieve. There's a destroyer standing by, and two tugs are on the port side holding us up. They're going to try to save you—and that means saving the ship."

Another voice, unfamiliar, came in: "We've checked the deck above you, and it's under only about four and a half feet of water. We've sent word to the supply ship to build a coffer-dam. We'll put it on your overhead, pump the water out and cut through."

It was a long time before I got any more news. Meanwhile the oily water had risen to my waist, and the coughing was making me steadily thirstier, weaker, sicker. I must have passed out again, for when I came to I noticed that the ship was now on an almost even keel. My elation was short-lived, though.

"I'm sorry, Lee," came Bill's voice. "The coffer-dam didn't work. There was no way to get through the overhead without drowning you."

"I was afraid of that."

Now despair overwhelmed me. But after a few minutes Bill came back on again. "Lee, they've found a way to pump out the little fire-room next to Radio 3. They think they can cut through to you from there."

I waited by the bulkhead, listening for sounds of the rescue squad. Bill helped to pass the time by talking—about the good times we'd had, about our plans to go into business together. But a lot of time was going by. "What's taking them so long?" I asked angrily. "They can't *do* it, can they?"

"Take it easy," Bill said patiently. "They're in there. Put your hand against the bulkhead."

I moved my hand along the metal. Finally I felt a spot at about eye level that was getting warm. Gradually it grew pink, then red. Seconds later the red-hot spot became a cascade of sparks. They were through!

Suddenly the whole room blazed up in a blinding flash. The sparks had ignited the oil on the water! I screamed for them to stop. Ducking under the water, I fished up my blanket and threw it in front of me. It smothered the flames.

Again I wanted to cry. I stood there panting, up to my armpits in water, knowing I couldn't go on. I was spent, scorched inside and out. My head was light, and I felt that I was going to pass out again. Only this time I wouldn't get up.

"Hey!" someone shouted from the other side of the bulkhead. "We've got a hole big as a cigarette now. D'you want some water?" In a minute a tube was passed through, and I was drinking my fill.

"I feel fine now," I announced. "Let's get to work."

The bulkhead was four inches thick, but the cutting job went fairly fast. At last the rescue squad pronounced the hole finished. It didn't look big enough, but it was now or never.

I looked at the sharp, jagged edges, took a deep breath, put my hands over my head and squeezed my shoulders carefully into the hole. Gently, the rescuers started dragging me through. As the steel cut into me, they stopped hauling for a moment. But as I saw the first human faces I had seen for 20 hours I forgot all about the pain. "Pull!" I begged. They did.

When I appeared on deck, black from head to foot with soot and oil, a cheer went up from the sailors. I was taken to the sick bay, where there were men wrapped like mummies in thick bandages with the blood soaking through. Chaplain Sharkey left them and came over to me. "They're glad you made it,

Lee," said the chaplain. "They were worried about you."

"But they look as though they're dying."

"They are."

I sat in silence while my cuts were dressed and the oil was cleaned off. Then I left the sick bay and walked along the deck, which was full of dead and wounded. I glanced over at the supply ship, the destroyers, the tugs and ships out in the misty harbour that had postponed the war long enough to come to my rescue.

Peace Pact

When I asked a friend of mine what was the secret of her long and happy marriage, she said, "Early in our marriage my husband and I discovered that there was no subject on which we could reach an agreement. And so . . . we've never tried!" .
—Contributed by Barbara Steel

*   *   *

Candid Shots

Leaving a boxing arena after an exciting bout, a spectator remarked to his companion: "Gosh, what a fight it must have been on television!"
—*S.I.*

One woman to another: "We're trying to enlarge our circle of friends to include people we like."
—*T.O.M.*

A father whose son managed to get through school and into the Army without absorbing even the rudiments of spelling, punctuation or penmanship observed ruefully: "When Ted writes home, his letters look and sound exactly like ransom notes."
—Contributed by Sydnia Gilmore

Woman to lunch companion: "Listen very carefully, because I can only tell this once—I promised not to repeat it."
—Mike Connolly

One young thing to another: "He's as nutty as a fruit cake, and I'll give him to you for Christmas."

In an hotel ladies' room, four matrons were searching in their purses for change when one of them said, "No, Myrtle, you took us to lunch. This is my treat."
—Contributed by Helen Potter

A glamorous girl was bragging about all the jewels that her admirers had given her. "The trouble with her," remarked a rival, "is that she's getting too big for her brooches."
—H. G.

Humour in Uniform

IT IS a tradition in many U.S. Army regiments that parents of a child born while the father is assigned to a regiment be presented by the other officers with a silver baby cup suitably engraved with the baby's name, birth date and regimental identification.

In 1954 the officers of the U.S. Army research board met for an annual regimental social gathering. Baby cups were presented to several new parents—one of them went to a British lieutenant-colonel, a liaison officer.

Feeling called upon to make an acceptance speech, he said, "I'm very pleased to receive this cup, but I must say it's the first time I've ever been awarded a trophy for this particular sport!" —L. L. ELDER

LANDING A JET plane on the rolling deck of an aircraft carrier can be tricky business. On one of my brother's first flights as a radar-man aboard a naval jet, he gave the radar fix to the pilot, indicating the plane's position above the carrier deck preparatory to landing. But the pilot, also a novice at carrier flying, continued to circle the deck.

My brother again gave him the radar fix, but the pilot continued to circle. Somewhat upset, my brother peeped into the cockpit. To his consternation, he found the pilot reading the manual of landing instructions. —ANN GERMANO

A SIGN on the entrance of a naval sick bay, instructing personnel how to obtain emergency treatment after hours, went into lengthy detail as to where a sick-berth attendant might be found, how to contact him and what to do until he arrived. Then came the last line: "If you have had time to read these instructions, your case is not an emergency. Come back tomorrow." —ROBERT FALLS

UPON LEARNING that he had been promoted to brigadier, my husband telephoned his 81-year-old mother to tell her the exciting news. "Oh, how lovely!" she exclaimed. Then she added, after a moment's pause, in a suddenly worried voice, "Dear?"

"Yes, mother?"

"Weren't you *happy* as a colonel?" —MRS. N. R. J.

BEFORE BEING shipped overseas, a group of us, all under 21 and greenhorns at that, decided to sample the port's night life. We started out at a plush spot. The waiter came to take our orders, which we all gave with a worldly air—except for one fellow who gave us all away. His order? "A Scotch and whisky, please." —M. W. STERLING

ON A REPORT in a Canadian Army file is this comment by a senior officer: "This report is useless. The only thing to remember of it is the identity of the officer who wrote it!" —G. T. J. BARRETT

A Reader's Digest
"First Person" Award

Typhoon

For nine hours the destroyer
was out of control in that fearful storm.
Something kept her afloat—some kind of miracle

By Captain Charles Calhoun, U.S.N., as told to John Hubbell

COLD, BLACK and alive with weather, the Philippine Sea was writhing, heaving, steadily mounting. It was nearly dusk on December 17, 1944. All day Task Force 38 of Admiral William "Bull" Halsey's Third Fleet—destroyers, cruisers and carriers which had been hammering Japanese installations on Luzon—had been replenishing its ammunition, food and fuel from our support force in a rendezvous at sea.

In that weather it had taken superb seamanship to avoid collisions. Fuelling hoses had come adrift again and again. Now, with night falling fast, the order came to secure until dawn.

Conning my destroyer, the U.S.S. *Dewey,* to her station where she would be part of a circular anti-submarine screen for the support force, I felt a sense of foreboding. I had seen rough seas in the North Atlantic, but nothing like those that were building up round us. We were in the centre of an ocean belt which is raked by savage typhoons. Obviously one was going to hit us hard—and fast.

Already the *Dewey* was groaning as she heaved and pitched drunkenly in the heightening seas. Needing more weight down in the hold, I ordered the fresh water and fuel to be shifted from high to low tanks, and ammunition moved from the ready-use boxes down into the magazines. All hands lashed and stowed everything movable. By 2 a.m. the *Dewey* was riding as though caught in some giant washing machine. But she was stable, and as tight as she could be made.

With morning the sky greyed and endless mountains of water ran towards all horizons. The wind was a hell's chorus of fury, whip-lashing clouds of spray and spume across the sea. Visibility was barely half a mile. No thought of refuelling now. Just stay afloat.

"Man · overboard!" The word came by radio from one ship, then another. I heard it 20 times in an hour. I went to the public-address system and warned all hands: "Rescue in these seas is virtually impossible. Every man who is not performing an essential job on deck must stay below."

The *Dewey* pounded on into the raging seas. She would bury her nose in the base of a gigantic swell, climb 50 feet or more to the crest, expose her keel as far back as the bridge, then throw her screws and half her bottom clear as she plunged deep into the trough. On each pitch she took a solid wall of water aboard, often over the bridge.

Suddenly we were in trouble. The radar showed a ship bearing down fast on our starboard bow.

"Steer one-three-zero!" I shouted. The *Dewey* lurched into a sharp turn. She was in the trough of the sea now, rolling between heaving cliffs of water but driving ahead, towards the centre of the support force. Finally, at the top of a huge swell I saw the oncoming ship, the *Monterey*. She was passing 500 yards to starboard. Now I could turn back on station.

"Steer one-eight-zero." Nothing happened. I glanced at the helmsman, saw him fighting the wheel, a look of desperate surprise on his face.

"She's not answering, sir." I was on a collision course with the centre of the support force and running out of ocean!

"Right full rudder! Port engine ahead full!" But the *Dewey* wouldn't budge. Nor would she turn more than 20 degrees in the opposite direction. We were "in irons"—caught in so strong a vice of wind and sea that our 50,000-horse-power engines were helpless.

I grabbed my radio-telephone and, using the *Dewey's* code name, told the support force: *"This is Achilles. I am out of control, crossing through the formation from starboard to port. Keep clear!"*

There was actually little the support-force skippers could do except hope that we would miss their ships. Should one of them turn to avoid us, he risked collision with the adjacent column, turning the formation into a tragic mêlée.

We wallowed close to a big tanker. A tremendous swell picked us up and threw us towards it, but suddenly we were past the tanker and heading for a cargo vessel. I could almost have reached out and touched it. Some muttered prayer on the bridge was heard, and we got past the cargo ship too. The radarscope showed two more columns of vessels to cross. It seemed impossible that we could evade the high, sharp prow of at least one of them. We were certain to be split in half! But twice more we came within spitting distance of huge tankers and weren't touched. Then at last we were in the clear.

I tried to regain control. No use. Sledge-hammered by the sea, the ship was starting to roll violently. She was staying heeled over longer than I liked, and there was a vagueness, a wishy-washy punch-drunkenness about the way she was coming back. For the first time it occurred to me that we might capsize.

Salt spray was being driven through the wheel-house with such force that it was actually peeling paint and clawing its way into watertight instruments, putting them out of commission. Signalmen, huddled near the wing of the bridge scanning the sea for other ships, turned back into the wheel-house, their faces raw and bleeding.

We were rolling so steeply to starboard now that when we grabbed the overhead stanchions our feet were coming clear of the deck. I watched the inclinometer. The ship was heeling over to 40 degrees . . . coming back . . . heeling to 42 degrees . . . coming back . . . but never all the way back, and more slowly each time.

I worried about my engines. In the after engine room, each roll to starboard dropped the level of lubricating oil below the suction point, stopping oil flow to the engine. If the engine was not stopped when we started each roll it would be ruined, and the instant we lost engine power we were finished. It was a delicate job that needed superb timing and co-ordination. I thanked God for chief machinist's mate Dorwin Hill; I knew that he could handle the problem if anyone could.

What I didn't know was that the storm had ripped open the forward fireroom airlock hatch, admitting some 500 to 1,000 gallons of sea water. While the fireroom gang worked frantically, sometimes shoulder-deep in water, Andrew Tolmie, the chief water tender, struggled over blistering hot steam lines and up a ladder to the flooded airlock. The seas in the lock smashed at him furiously. Dazed and bruised, he climbed to the top, reached the outer hatch and locked it.

There was quiet tension on the bridge. I knew what the men were thinking. Each roll to starboard was greater than the last. We stayed over longer each time. How far could she go, and recover?

"Frank, do you recall the ship's stability curves?" I asked my executive officer, Lieutenant-Commander Frank Bampton.

"She's supposed to recover from 70 degrees, Captain." I had never heard of a ship recovering from such a roll; the idea seemed preposterous.

Now came another giant roll to starboard. The quartermasters and signalmen swung like pendulums from overhead grips. They were nearly parallel to the deck. The inclinometer needle showed 68 . . . 69 . . . 70 degrees! The *Dewey* had lost. Any second now we would be buried with her for ever.

"O God, please make her come back!" someone prayed. Slowly, almost imperceptibly, the *Dewey* inched back, riding erratically like a car on flat tyres.

Another lunge to starboard, 72 degrees this time. She stayed over for two interminable minutes, then came wallowing back. And now another roll, the worst yet. The inclinometer needle hit its limit at 75 degrees, and still we kept rolling, nearly to our beam-ends. This *had* to be the finish—no ship can sail on its side! I could see the men round me praying.

We were nearly turned over now, in the deepest valley of water I had ever seen. Another inch or two would do it. But we stayed on our beam, rode to the top of the advancing mountain of water and gradually began righting ourselves.

How long could the *Dewey* last? How much could she take? There seemed no end to this storm. The barometer needle was off the scale.

Suddenly the half-inch-thick guy wire which ran from the deck to support the forward funnel parted and snapped past my ear like a rifle shot. The funnel crumpled slowly like a huge empty sock across the starboard side of the ship, knocking away a whaler and its heavy davits. Smoke billowed out of the gaping hole in the deck and steam roared out of a broken line.

The *Dewey* shivered upright. She had a new feeling of stability. She still kept heeling to starboard but not so far, and she snapped back quickly. Loss of the towering weight of the funnel and reduction of area for the wind to push against, plus loss of the whaler and its davits from the starboard side, had done the trick.

"Barometer has started to go up, sir."

We had been in the typhoon proper for five hours. I calculated that we were close to the eye of the storm— about half-way through. We had some rough sailing ahead, but I knew we were going to make it.

We came out of it abruptly at 6 p.m. One moment we were in a clawing, impenetrable fog of spray and spume; the next, we were in the clear. The seas were still enormous but the wind fell off to 50 knots. I rang down "half ahead" and the *Dewey* answered her rudder. For the first time in nine hours, I had her under control. The *Dewey* had made it.

THE NEXT morning we learned of the typhoon's dreadful toll. The Task Force had lost 790 officers and men—lost overboard, killed at their stations or trapped in their sunken ships; 80 more had been badly injured; three destroyers had capsized and been lost, with only a handful of survivors; two others had been wounded at least as severely as the *Dewey;* one cruiser and four carriers had all suffered major damage, and 146 aircraft had been lost or damaged beyond repair. A score of other vessels had suffered lesser injuries. Of the disaster, Admiral Chester Nimitz, Commander-in-Chief of the Pacific Fleet, said it was "the greatest loss we have taken in the Pacific, without compensatory return, since the first Battle of Savo."

An earnest discussion was in progress on the *Dewey's* bridge. "What do you think brought us through,

sir? We didn't lose a man and nobody was badly hurt."

I thought of the way the engine-room and fireroom watches had reacted. I remembered the way each prayer from the bridge had been answered at just the right time—and the way the stack had collapsed at the last moment before what was certain to be our final roll.

"A great crew saved us," I said. "That, and some kind of miracle, I suppose."

"There's your miracle, sir." A sailor was pointing aloft.

The port yardarm, made of three-inch steel pipe, was bent *upwards!* There was no reason for it. Even when we had heeled over 75 degrees, that yardarm could not have touched the water. It was as though some Great Hand had reached down and pulled the *Dewey* up, just as she was about to capsize.

We left the yardarm in that position for a long time. It gave us all on the *Dewey* a feeling of reassurance as we prepared for battle.

A Regular Tonic

WHENEVER I get depressed, I take from my wallet an old scrap of paper with an unusual shopping list on it. This was the list my wife and I made 20 years ago when I was asked to accept an important job in the city. We wrote down all the things we wanted in life: a pleasant home, good friends, health for the family, frequent opportunity to enjoy the outdoor life we both loved. We discovered that we already had all these things and we agreed that the move would not enhance them. A look at the shopping list of solid verities is the greatest tonic I know for the blues, and fortunately every one of us can compile a similar list of his own blessings. —J. C. C.

*More than £2 million lay at the
bottom of the bay, and the Japanese
were determined to get it all. They
tried hard, but they reckoned without
the resourcefulness of some of their
reluctant employees*

The Affair of the Vanishing Pesos

By John Hubbell

IN THE LATE summer of 1942, when
the Japanese had been in control
of the Philippines for several months,
their occupation currency suddenly
began to collapse. Japanese soldiers
found that a month's pay wouldn't
buy so much as a glass of beer. The
cause was a mysterious flood of silver

Philippine pesos that began turning up in the markets of Manila.

Somehow the silver was reaching even the prisoner-of-war camps. American prisoners were bribing demoralized Japanese guards for food, clothing and medicine. Next, they would start buying freedom! If the source of the silver wasn't found soon, it could corrupt the whole structure of Japanese control.

Where did the silver come from? The Japanese knew that the MacArthur forces had dumped millions of pesos into the deep water south of Corregidor before surrendering. There was more than £2,000,000 of it down there, lying at a depth of 120 feet. A diving crew of seven American prisoners of war had been put to work salvaging that fortune—it would be a gift from the army to the emperor. Japanese security police were watching the American divers, guarding every peso recovered. It seemed inconceivable that any of this silver could be smuggled into Manila. Nevertheless, the Japanese decided to tighten the guard over the Americans.

IT HAD ALL started in the early months of 1942, when defeat in the Philippines had become inevitable. Quickly Philippine government officials and U.S. Army officers decided to save the Philippine national treasury. They recorded the serial numbers of hundreds of millions of pounds' worth of paper currency, then burned the notes. In February,

some £500,000 in gold bullion and £90,000 in silver were shipped to San Francisco in the ballast tanks of a submarine. But now time and the enemy were moving fast. There was no way to get out the rest of the treasury: 17 million silver pesos (each worth half a crown) still lay packed in wooden boxes in a steel vault on Corregidor.

On April 20, U.S. Army officers drew two straight lines connecting well-known landmarks of Manila Bay on a map. The lines intersected at a point in the water on Caballo Bay, formed by the thin crescent of Corregidor's curled tail. There the water was deep and rough enough to discourage enemy salvage. There the treasure would be dumped.

Lieutenant-Commander George Harrison, commanding harbour craft in near-by Mariveles Bay, gathered up a working party. Most of them were divers. Harrison told them that Corregidor's days were numbered; the job had to be done quickly and at night.

It took ten nights to move the 425 tons of silver to the bottom of Caballo Bay. When the job was finished Harrison turned the men loose with a prophetic warning: "If you are captured, don't let them find out you are divers."

On May 6, Corregidor surrendered. The divers were among those captured. Six weeks later the Japanese commandant of the prison camp at Cabanatuan, 90 miles north of

Manila, sent for Bosun's Mate First Class Morris "Moe" Solomon. "We know you are a diver," he said. "Manila harbour is choked with sunken vessels. It must be cleared for traffic."

The Japanese had excellent intelligence. Besides Solomon, they had singled out Bosun's Mates Virgil "Jughead" Sauers, Wallace "Punchy" Barton, P. L. "Slim" Mann and two other experienced divers.

Before leaving Cabanatuan, the group sought out Lieutenant-Commander Frank Davis, who had been their skipper. "You know what they are really after," Davis said. "Don't let them get it!"

The men knew that if the Japanese sent them down for the silver, they would have to bring some up or be shot. But they agreed they would deliver only enough to stall the enemy. They would steal as much as they could, and smuggle it to other American prisoners to bribe guards for food and medicine. One thing seemed certain: sooner or later they would be caught and executed for sabotage. But this was war, and here was a chance to do the enemy expensive damage.

On the train to Manila the enemy's stern attitude changed. Smiling guards gave each man pork sandwiches and cigarettes. In Manila they were ushered to a clean room in a building near the docks. There was a locker and a bed for each of them. They were Very Important Prisoners indeed!

A Japanese civilian in a seedy-looking suit entered. He wore a horseshoe of greyish hair around his bald head, thick glasses and a huge smile. He looked like an actor in a bad spy-film; but his voice, soft and high-pitched, was friendly.

"I am Mr. Yosobe," he said. "We will be working together. I am a little too old for diving, but I have had 20 years' experience in salvage work. Come and meet our officer-in-charge."

Captain Takiuti greeted them on the dock. A pleasant, youngish man, he came from a wealthy Japanese family and spoke perfect English. He told the men they would be given a roomy boat to live on at Corregidor, and were to make themselves comfortable.

"No one will molest you," he promised. "There will be no guards. You are to consider yourselves on professional assignment." He said they would be working in shallow water—only 30 to 40 feet.

Obviously, Takiuti was lying. The enemy could make them do shallow-water work at gunpoint. This would be no ordinary job; otherwise the Japanese would not try to soft-soap them.

"Well, he called us professionals," Jughead Sauers said that night. "We'll have to charge some big professional fees—in silver!"

The next morning Yosobe and two Japanese guards showed the men the U.S. Navy diving gear which the Japanese had found:

several shallow-water helmets and two dozen suits of long, heavy diving underwear. It would be dangerous work. Should the weighted helmet tilt more than 45 degrees, it would fill with water and drown the diver. Shallow-water equipment was not designed to withstand the pressures below 36 feet. Moreover, the air hoses to these helmets were at least ten years old and might collapse when a man was on the bottom.

The men didn't like the look of the equipment. Nor did they like the 60-foot boat they were to live on— an old bucket tied to Corregidor's North Pier. The cabin was already serving as a dormitory for six Filipinos, hired to tend the Filipino divers who had been salvaging boxes of silver for the Japanese since the end of May. Eighteen boxes— £13,500 in silver—had been recovered. The Filipino divers, the Americans learned, had never worked in deep water before. They had stayed down too long, come up too fast. Two had died in the agony of the "bends." When a third lost his helmet and failed to come up, the survivors refused to dive, and the Japanese sent them to prison.

That night the Americans discussed the situation. Those first 18 boxes of silver proved that the rest could be recovered; this sharpened the enemy's greed. Obviously, the Japanese Army wanted full credit for salvaging the silver. Otherwise, Imperial Navy divers would have been used. This explained why they were so anxious for the co-operation of the Americans. Perhaps they would make more concessions.

When Takiuti appeared, the divers told him that the boat they lived on was a pigsty. It needed cleaning, paint and repair. Men who worked at such hazardous duty, they said, deserved pleasant, relaxing quarters.

"Help yourself to whatever you can find on the island," Takiuti told the startled prisoners.

From Corregidor's rubble the sailors scrounged a lush harvest. In a few days the barge, scrubbed and painted, began to look like a pleasure yacht.

They were just beginning to enjoy domestic life when Yosobe spoilt it all. Early one morning he arrived with two Japanese soldiers and hustled the Americans and the Filipino tenders aboard a small fishing boat. They chugged slowly round the east end of Corregidor, then pointed towards Caballo Bay. In the distance the Americans saw a flat diving barge. It was anchored directly over the place where they had dumped the treasure!

In a few minutes a motor launch approached and put a big, tough-looking, impassive Japanese aboard the diving barge. His uniform showed that he was a *Kempei*—a member of the Japanese Military Police. An ordinary soldier might be bribed, but a *Kempei,* they knew, was incorruptible, intelligent and answerable to no one for his actions.

He could shoot them on the spot, no questions asked.

The *Kempei's* first act was to end the sham that they would be salvaging sunken ships. He spoke to Yosobe in Japanese. "Your orders are to salvage the silver dumped here before the surrender," Yosobe said to the Americans, smiling. The divers had planned to tell Yosobe they knew nothing of such silver. But a look at the *Kempei* changed their minds. They did, however, tell Yosobe their diving plans. They would spend only 15 minutes at a time on the bottom. Coming up, they would decompress for two minutes at 30 feet, three minutes at 20 feet, eight minutes at ten feet.

"Surely you can work longer than 15 minutes a dive," Yosobe argued.

"That's plenty of time with this gear," Sauers said. "You've lost three divers already. You want to kill us?"

Yosobe, a gentle man, had vivid memories of the way the Filipino divers had died, and he did not want to see those death agonies again. He shrugged.

The Americans fastened a 40-foot length of cable to a bollard, tied loops in it ten feet apart and dropped it over the side. They would stand in the loops while decompressing.

A small, flat vessel stood alongside the barge. A thick cable from a hand winch ran over its deck and hung down towards the water. There was a belt-like strap at the end. When a diver found a box of silver, he was to loop this strap round it and two Filipinos would winch it up.

Sauers was to make the first dive. He got into the helmet, ran the air hose and lifeline beneath his right arm and grabbed the cable strap. Then he let himself down into the water.

It was warm and calm. Slowly, carefully, Sauers inched his way down the descending line, a thick Manila rope anchored to the bottom. The deeper he travelled, the darker and colder it got. Soon he stood motionless on the firm, sandy bottom. Then the ocean floor came into focus, and he saw it!

A towering mountain of boxes lay some yards from him. If the enemy had the slightest hint that the silver was so concentrated he would permit no delay. Competent divers could bring the entire fortune to the surface in a few weeks.

Sauers thought hard: since the Filipinos had already brought up 18 boxes, the Japanese knew they were in the right spot. It would be best to send up a few boxes at once to prove the divers' reliability and give them more time to plan.

A 20-foot circling line was attached to the bottom of the descending line. Sauers tied it round his waist and moved slowly towards the hill of silver. He looped the lifting cable round a box and gave three tugs—the signal to the Filipinos to haul it up.

Fifteen minutes later he climbed

aboard the barge. When he got his helmet off, Sauers began to grin. Yosobe and the *Kempei* were paying no attention to him. Both were on the smaller vessel, standing over the sweating Filipinos, ordering them to move the box of silver to the rear of the boat. The *Kempei* stationed himself next to it and indicated that he would guard it with his life. This concern of the Japanese for the silver rather than the divers was to prove their big mistake.

Solomon made the next dive, and sent up a box. Barton made a third dive but sent nothing up. "Couldn't find a damn thing down there," he told Yosobe.

"But the others found boxes," Yosobe pleaded.

"They must've got all there was around here," Punchy replied airily.

"We will try again," Yosobe said. But it was now shortly after noon, when the waters of the bay began to grow choppy.

"We can't dive any more today," Sauers told him. "This water is too rough. Do you want to kill us?"

Yosobe did not want to kill them. Diving ceased for the day, and they headed back to the living-barge.

Captain Takiuti met them at the North Pier with a ham and a bottle of whisky. Only 12,000 pesos had been recovered but it was a promising start. They would begin working in earnest tomorrow.

On their living-barge, the Americans cooked dinner and made plans. They had noticed that the two boxes

they had sent up were waterlogged and beginning to rot. On future dives they would loosen the ends so that the heavy bags of silver would break out and spill as the box was being lifted. Then they would steal the loose silver.

Moe Solomon cut up several pairs of dungarees and sewed the trouser legs into bags fitted with drawstrings and a cord to tie round the diver's waist. The bag would hang under his diving underwear. On the bottom, the diver would fill his bag with pesos and as he came aboard his tenders would remove it and hide it beneath raincoats on deck.

Slim Mann dived first. Secreted beneath his diving underwear he had a marlinespike for breaking open the boxes. On the bottom, he stripped the metal bands from one box and prised at both ends until they seemed loose. Then he signalled and watched it rise.

About half-way to the surface the box collapsed and bags of silver came drifting down. The Filipinos felt the weight slip away and lowered the cable again. Mann attached another ruined box and it too burst. Then he stabbed the marlinespike into the ocean bed and went up.

There was consternation on the barge. Yosobe was frantic. What had happened to the silver? The *Kempei* stood close by, silent, staring angrily.

"This is going to be a helluva job!" Sauers shouted with feigned disgust. "Those boxes are rotten.

Fall apart when you touch 'em."

"But two boxes arrived yesterday all right," Yosobe said.

"We were lucky yesterday," Mann replied. "Look at the boxes we've got. They are full of water rot."

Barton dived next. He stuffed as many of the loose pesos as he could carry into the sack beneath his diving underwear, then sent up an undamaged box to appease Yosobe. He reached the surface as the box was being lifted aboard the smaller vessel. While the Japanese were inspecting it, Solomon untied his money bag and slipped it into a bucket beneath a raincoat.

Moe Solomon went down next

and sent Yosobe another undamaged box. Then he shattered a dozen boxes and dumped the silver on to the ocean bed. This would make it easier to get at the pesos on the dives to follow.

That night the Americans counted their loot: 1,500 pesos. To buy off any suspicious Japanese, and set up a distribution system to get the silver to American prisoners on Corregidor and in Manila, they would need much more. "Gentlemen, we must do better!" Punchy Barton said, and they did.

In the next two weeks the Americans stuffed 20,000 silver pesos, worth £2,500, into the bilges of the living-barge. The enemy's take was

110,000 pesos. It wasn't enough to satisfy Yosobe. He decided that the job was going too slowly. The only answer was to find more divers.

At Cabanatuan prison camp the Japanese picked out three other experienced U.S. divers: Torpedo-man Robert Sheats, Bosun's Mate George Chopchick and Carpenter's Mate H. S. Anderson. All of them were old shipmates of the divers in Caballo Bay.

49

When they came on board the old hands explained the set-up, then showed them the living quarters. The newcomers were flabbergasted. Nooks and crevices were filled with tobacco, sweets, peanuts, salt, sugar, pepper, eggs, coffee, rum.

Sheats, Anderson and Chopchick gleefully counted the take—2,430 pesos that day. Afterwards they helped to carry it through a trapdoor down to a dark lower deck. The divers hauled at long lines through the bilge hatches. Bucketfuls of silver arrived at the hatch openings.

Then the old hands explained how the system worked. The Filipinos who manned the air pumps were allowed to visit their families in Manila. The Americans had studied them carefully, tested them with derogatory remarks about the Emperor of Japan. Finally, convinced of their loyalty, they told them that they were stealing silver. Would the Filipinos help to distribute it? They would.

The pump hands found some Chinese money-changers in Manila who were glad to exchange Japan's paper occupation currency for Philippine silver—at a black-market rate that undermined the yen. Ultimately they got so much silver into circulation in Manila that the rate of exchange fell drastically and nobody would have anything to do with the Japanese occupation currency. The money was used to buy supplies, or smuggled to American prisoners of war. The Filipinos helped themselves to large commissions. The Americans felt they deserved it. They were risking their lives.

The day after Sheats and Chopchick arrived, Yosobe had the living boat towed to the South Pier, closer to the treasure site, to speed up the work. The divers didn't like it, for there would be no privacy here. A tug and an enemy barge were tied on either side of them. The Japanese sailors were likely to inspect the living-barge on a moment's whim. But that day, at least, they would be too busy. Skies were darkening and seas were running high. The sailors were making ready for a storm.

By next morning the area was in the shrieking, maniacal grip of a fully-fledged typhoon. The whole South China Sea seemed to be marching into Manila Bay in endless processions of gigantic waves. The Japanese sailors abandoned the tug for shelter in Corregidor's tunnels. But the Americans had to save their boat. It was old and wooden; if it smashed against the rocky shore it would inevitably spill its forbidden cargo on to the beaches.

For hours, Slim Mann and Jughead Sauers rode the ancient bucket against the howling fury of the storm. Every few minutes they felt the hull crack and shudder as it slammed against the bottom of Caballo Bay in the trough between waves. Fearing that the old barge would break loose from its mooring, they threw coils of thick line and cable to the other divers on the pier, who lashed them to bollards. As the lines and cables snapped like strings, Mann or Sauers would hurl more line to the pier.

By some miracle of effort they held on. When the typhoon was finally past, Corregidor was a shambles. Not a tree was left standing. The Japanese barge had been carried away. Dozens of boxes of silver had been lifted from the watery vault far out in the bay and smashed open on the island's south shore, where Filipino workers were eagerly helping themselves. But the living-barge was still tied to the pier.

After the storm, working parties of prisoners were brought out to clean up the mess. The working parties weren't heavily guarded, and the enemy soldiers couldn't tell a diver from any other prisoner. Two or three at a time, the divers moved into a group and started working. When the guards weren't looking, they passed the silver to the startled POW's. Soon the divers had delivered thousands of pesos. They decided not to press their luck further, and it was as well they didn't, for the next morning Captain Takiuti came aboard.

With Takiuti was a smaller, vicious-looking officer. They moved slowly through the cabin, poked at mattresses, looked beneath piles of diving underwear, into the medicine cabinet, the stove and the bookcases. So the enemy suspected them! Finally, Takiuti stood on the piece of carpet that covered the trapdoor to the lower level. Takiuti knew of the hold. There were still thousands of pesos in the bilges. The divers thought the game was up.

But Takiuti surprised them. "You men must make better progress in recovering the silver," he said severely. Then, unaccountably, he turned and left.

"He must have forgotten the hold!" someone breathed.

"He didn't forget," Sauers said. "It was wet and filthy the last time he saw it. He probably didn't want to get dirty. They'll be back! Let's get that stuff out of here!"

They would have to return their hoard of silver to the sea.

One by one they took the buckets of silver out of the bilges, but it wasn't easy to get the buckets into the water. Japanese soldiers lined the dock, watching them work. If one of them spied a bucket going into the water, he might begin to wonder. So they kept their backs to the enemy troops, stayed in a tight semicircle around each diver until he got into the water. Then someone would hand the bucket down to him. Ten buckets of silver were laid on the bottom that day.

The next day Takiuti and three armed soldiers probed every inch of the living-barge. The divers followed them, expressions of outraged hurt on their faces.

"We've worked hard for you, Captain," Moe Solomon said earnestly. "Now you act as though we're *thieves* or something!"

"I think it is highly possible," Takiuti snapped, "that you *are* thieves —or something!" Takiuti was furious when he led his inspection party off the barge. He hadn't found a single peso. The divers knew they hadn't fooled him. He knew they were stealing the silver and was determined to find it. When he did, they would all be shot.

The next morning their fears were confirmed. As they prepared to dive, the *Kempei* suddenly appeared on the diving barge. He spoke in Japanese to Yosobe and began stripping.

"He is going to dive," Yosobe said. "He wants to see what you have been doing on the bottom."

The divers glanced at each other. This was the end for them all. The *Kempei* could not be allowed to return from the sea alive. But they too were doomed. The enemy would accept no excuse for a *Kempei's* death. The *Kempei* was fitted with a helmet and started to descend into the water. Sheats tended the lifeline, Barton the air hose. When the *Kempei* reached bottom, Sheats planned to rip the helmet from his head.

The *Kempei* grabbed the descending line and started down. But after moving only a few feet, he started up again! Out of the helmet, he went into a huddle with Yosobe.

"*Kempei* has claustrophobia," Yosobe explained to the divers. "He can't stand the helmet. And he has decided you have not been doing wrong on the bottom, or you would not have co-operated in sending him down." The old man was visibly relieved. The divers were weak.

The diving continued until late autumn, when the silver-recovery programme ended. By then it was obvious to the Japanese that the silver was coming from Caballo Bay. But they would never admit even to themselves that it had been stolen by the American divers. They could never have got past the *Kempeis!*

The security police now reported officially that all the silver in circulation had been taken from the boxes washed ashore in the typhoon. The case was closed. To keep it closed, they cancelled the silver-recovery programme, and everyone was happy, especially the Americans.

The divers were sent to Manila to work as stevedores in a group commanded by Lieutenant-Commander George Harrison, the man who had worked with them during the dumping of the silver. They spent the next two years with "Harrison's 400 Thieves," looting or sabotaging every enemy cargo of food and war supplies they could reach.

All the men survived the war except George Chopchick, who died in 1944 aboard a prison ship *en route* to Japan. None of them is rich. Sauers is the only one who can show so much as a single souvenir peso. But each often remembers his days of philanthropy in the summer and autumn of 1942.

"I suppose we were the richest prisoners of war ever," Sheats said recently. "It was pretty good duty.

We were like Snow White's seven dwarfs—carrying our buckets off to work each day, bringing them home filled with silver at night."

As for the silver, £625,000-worth was raised after the war, then the work ceased. The boxes kept crumbling and the effort became more expensive than the silver was worth.

In 1947, two Americans got a contract from the Philippine Government, but were able to raise only about another £60,000.

More than £1,000,000 in silver still lies scattered over Caballo Bay. It will probably remain there for ever—a watery monument to the men who did their best to keep it there.

The dramatic, human story of the invasion of France

THE LONGEST DAY

By Cornelius Ryan

THE GUARDIAN of Hitler's Atlantic Wall was going on leave. Tired and haggard, Rommel had decided that it would be safe to leave the front. The situation, he reported, "was not indicative that an invasion was imminent." Carrying a birthday present for his wife, Rommel climbed into his staff car and headed for Germany. *The date was June 4, 1944 . . .*

In a quiet bunker in Normandy, Lieutenant-Colonel Helmuth Meyer was flashing an urgent message to all German headquarters. The B.B.C. had broadcast a code message to the French Resistance—and Meyer knew it was a warning that the Invasion was imminent. The message should have alerted the defending forces, but each commander assumed that another had raised the alarm. So all along the Channel front, the defenders were relaxed. Lieutenant-General Speidel was planning a dinner party. Other senior officers began leaving for Rennes, for a tactical exercise. *It was now June 5, 1944 . . .*

At Allied Headquarters in Southern England, General Eisenhower's staff were gathered to make one of history's most fateful decisions. Already their plans had been bedevilled by weather; now they were to decide for the second time. A British general dressed in corduroys and a roll-neck sweater was quite sure of his view. "I would say—go," Montgomery said. *Tuesday, June 6, was to be D-Day . . .*

In Cornelius Ryan's brilliant reconstruction of one of the greatest events in modern history, both sides of the story are told—for the first time. This tense, gripping narrative is being presented exclusively in The Reader's Digest in two long instalments, beginning NEXT MONTH.

One of the best-kept secrets of the War was the location—
indeed the very existence—of the command post from which
Winston Churchill directed Britain to victory. Even now, few
people have seen this subterranean complex of Cabinet War
Rooms, the chief of which are equipped and furnished just as
they were during the Battle of Britain.

James Stewart-Gordon has written a compelling account
of the dramatic events that occurred in "This Secret Place,"
as Churchill called it. Interviews with the men and women who
worked there have revealed hitherto unpublished details about
significant war-time happenings.

Churchill's own courage, eccentricity and genius live on in
these underground chambers. His personality gives vivid colour
to this reconstruction.

"THIS SECRET PLACE"

by James Stewart-Gordon

THE CABINET War Rooms lie buried under the curlicued pile of a government building in Storey's Gate off Whitehall. More than 150 cell-like rooms, some no larger than a fox's den, open off a mile of corridors. They cover six acres, all beneath a 15-foot-thick slab of solid concrete. At the height of the war as many as 300 people worked in these cellars. To them it was "The Hole," or simply "down there." But to Winston Churchill it was "This Secret Place."

In these rooms in May 1940 Churchill declared, "If invasion comes this is where I shall sit." Pointing to his chair at the head of the Cabinet table, he said: "I shall sit there until either the Germans are driven back, or they carry me out dead."

No hint of this vast subterranean headquarters ever reached the

CROWN COPYRIGHT

The Map Room, where action on every war front was followed and recorded

enemy, yet it was here that every stratagem in the death-duel with Germany was debated, each stroke of war recorded. Here giant maps and charts, studded with coloured pins, marked the great land, sea and air battles. Here the magnificent hoaxes of "The Man Who Never Was" and "Monty's Double" were cooked up. Here, from his bed-sitter, Churchill made his historic broadcasts, and from a room no larger than a lavatory held his telephone conversations with President Roosevelt in Washington.

Today the bulk of the space has been converted into storerooms or

The building in Storey's Gate, off Whitehall, which houses the Cabinet War Rooms

abandoned to reverberating emptiness. But six of the rooms are preserved as a memorial. On the wall of the Prime Minister's bedroom, no longer concealed by the curtain which was its only wartime protection, hangs the most secret map which showed in detail every preparation against invasion. In the official Map Room, score was kept during the Battle of Britain of downed enemy and British aircraft, on a device like a Test Match scoreboard. The estimated score of the big day of the match, September 15, 1940, still stands on the board: Germany—downed 183, probable 42, damaged 75.

Near by is the Cabinet Room, whose table still holds the fading place cards: Mr. Bevin, Mr. Attlee, Lord Beaverbrook. It was here, in the blackest days of the war, that one of the most crucial meetings of the Cabinet was called. Churchill, who was in Cairo, had sent a request for a new commander in North Africa, where Rommel was piling up victory after victory. But the officer he asked for had already been appointed to General Eisenhower's staff in London.

The Cabinet debated the issue through the night until Ernest Bevin, the lights glinting on his pebble spectacles, the stub of a cigarette stuck to his lower lip, said, "We either have to send the man or propose an alternate. Since we don't have an alternate, we'll have to send the man Winston wants." The man, of course, was Montgomery, and his triumph over Rommel at El Alamein turned the tide in the war.

Less dramatically, it was also in "The Hole" that someone spotted, after scrutinizing a series of photographs, that Herr Hitler was subtly

with the German navy, it would knock out the Home Fleet. Hundreds of barges laden with Nazi soldiers were then to be towed and pushed across the English Channel. Once ashore, to eliminate the need to transport petrol, the troops would

The Cabinet Room

adding to his height by gradually increasing the size of his built-up heels.

And for outright comic relief, it was here in the summer of 1940 that a young officer came up with a sure-fire method of stopping Operation Sea Lion, Hitler's projected invasion of England. The German plan was first for the Luftwaffe to beat down the RAF. Next, in combination

mount bicycles for the final advance. The junior officer spoke up: "When they get ashore," he asked, "couldn't we just let the air out of their tyres?"

"If 'Itler Could 'Ear 'Im"

"THE HOLE" was first manned during the Munich Crisis; Chamberlain visited it on the day war was declared. But it was under

ALL COLOUR PHOTOGRAPHS FROM JACK LE VIEN'S PRODUCTION "THE FINEST HOURS"

Churchill that it assumed the air of urgency and excitement which a visitor can still feel today.*

"People call it Hitler's war," says one officer who served in This Secret Place. "It wasn't. Hitler may have started it, but after the tenth of May 1940, when he took over, it was Winston's war. He fought it with all the gusto of a fourth form schoolboy surrounded by his chums, putting paid to a bully. Of course they called this place the Cabinet War Room, but it was really Stalky and Co.'s cave—and Winston was Stalky."

Characteristically, soon after assuming his post as Prime Minister, Churchill made an inspection of his fortress. He arrived without warning, swept through the rooms, then asked for the exit that led most directly to No. 10 Downing Street. Guided to a little-used door, he stepped from the gloom into an English May morning. As if drawn by some invisible force a small knot of workmen materialized, and when Churchill moved through them, his stick pounding an *obbligato* to his firmly planted feet, they burst into an impromptu cheer. Smiling, but his eyes moist, he told a companion, "They trust me, and I can give them nothing but disaster for quite a long time."

The heart of "The Hole" consisted of the two main rooms: the

official Map Room, and the Cabinet Room. The latter is today, as it was then, a simple rectangular space filled with a series of tables set in the form of a hollow square. Crowded round the tables are the Ministers' chairs and at the centre of the table to the left of the door is an armchair, of the kind dentists have in their waiting-rooms. This was Churchill's. It was the decisions taken here which in the end were reflected in the victories and defeats shown on the walls of the Map Room.

When a Cabinet meeting was called here, Churchill entered first, and the others followed and took their places. To the Prime Minister's left were the members of his "kitchen cabinet," the gnome-like Lord Beaverbrook, the flaming-haired Brendan Bracken and occasionally "The Prof"—Professor F. E. Lindemann, later Lord Cherwell. Ernest Bevin sat on Churchill's right. On Churchill's immediate left was the Deputy Prime Minister, Clement Attlee, a quiet man with an inscrutable face, yet capable of moments of anger. These could be induced by any slight that he, an old infantry officer, felt was being placed on the Army.

After calling the meeting to order Churchill would bring up the first item on the agenda. The Minister whose department was concerned spoke and was then challenged. As argument began, voices rose. Churchill, revelling in the rough-and-tumble of debate, joined in until

---

* The Cabinet War Rooms may be visited only by special arrangement. Written applications should be sent to: The Chief Clerk, Cabinet Office, Whitehall, London S.W.1.

his voice, lustily intoning parliamentary phrases, drowned out the members of his Government.

Although the room was soundproofed, a small grille covered by wire netting had been left open. If there was a large difference of opinion the sound-level climbed until it overflowed through the grille. During one roaring interval, a Royal Marine on duty remarked: "If 'Itler could 'ear 'im, 'e'd belt up and run."

During these gales, the secretaries took down the Cabinet decisions in long-hand, and at the close of the meeting dashed off to dictate the results to typists. The reports were then rushed off for duplicating. Since Churchill was a man who was at his best after 5 p.m., he often called his Cabinet meetings late at night. It was a point of pride that, throughout the entire war, no matter at what hour the typists got the reports, a copy of the proceedings of the previous night was on each Minister's breakfast table by morning.

In the Cabinet Room, Churchill—who in addition to being Prime Minister had named himself as Minister of Defence—conferred also with the Chiefs of Staff. Although there were only the three chiefs, Sir Alan Brooke for the Army, Sir Dudley Pound for the Royal Navy and Sir Charles Portal for the RAF, and the secretariat, these sessions greatly resembled the Cabinet meetings in point of decibels,

firmness of purpose and debate.

Air Marshal Portal used to state his views succinctly and quietly, but Sir Alan Brooke, a slight man with long arms, had a rush of speech in which words tumbled over each other, like a river in spate, and sometimes managed to get mixed up in the process. Once he spent half an hour detailing a military position near Iran, which he kept referring to as Germany. When an *aide* tried to prompt him, Brooke snapped: "Don't correct me, you know damn well what I mean!" Admiral Pound on the other hand always appeared to be dozing until the word "Navy" was mentioned, but then he came awake with a rush, firing broadsides of argument and opinion.

Meanwhile, Churchill, who had his own views on military matters, sat in his chair like a swordsman facing the Three Musketeers singlehanded, laying about him in all directions at once.

Clement Attlee, Deputy Prime Minister of the wartime Government

An American observer, unused to the ancient British custom of loud and simultaneous debate, left one such session with his head reeling. "It was like the Tea Party in *Alice in Wonderland*," he said, "except that the Mad Hatter kept on turning into the March Hare!"

The Nerve Centre

IN CONTRAST to the Cabinet Room, the Map Room carried on its work in comparative silence. The atmosphere was, however, charged with tension, particularly during the great naval engagements — the *Graf Spee,* the *Bismarck,* the hunting of the *Scharnhorst* and the *Gneisenau.*

Then, as the positions of ships and planes were changed, almost as the action transpired, the room filled up and everyone seemed to hold his breath.

"You could almost hear the flash of the guns and the blast of the torpedoes," says a civil servant who was there. "After the *Bismarck* was sunk, I went outside and it wasn't until I started to cross Whitehall that I realized my legs were trembling so that I was scarcely able to walk."

Like the other underground rooms, the Map Room's roof is propped up with giant baulks of timber to support the vast weight of the concrete slab designed to make This Secret Place bombproof. These pillars add to the illusion that the room is a battle headquarters deep in the vitals of a warship.

Down the centre of the room are two long tables, still littered with

The Chiefs of Staff: Sir Alan Brooke, Sir Dudley Pound, Sir Charles Portal

yellowing papers detailing events of a quarter of a century ago. On top of each table is a raised shelf filled with red, white and green telephones, equipped with flashing lights instead of bells, and scrambling devices. These were used by watch officers of the three Services, none below the rank of lieutenant-colonel

leather-covered dispatch boxes, each bearing a crown. One is dirty black and labelled "The Cabinet and Committee of Imperial Defence." The other, faded red, is labelled "The King." These were delivered daily to Buckingham Palace and to the Prime Minister's office.

From September 1939, when the

The Map Room nerve centre

or its equivalent, who sat there receiving direct reports from their headquarters, by phone and by compressed-air tubes, and passing the information on to the officers manning the gigantic wall maps.

Facing the two tables is a desk, once occupied by a colonel who correlated the reports from each Service. Still on the desk are two

Polish and German armies, translated into rows of red- and black-topped pins stuck into maps, faced each other, the Map Room was always the eye of the hurricane. As word of the gallant but hopeless surge of Polish lancers against German tanks and self-propelled cannon reached the room, the red-topped pins representing Polish units were moved forward towards the black-topped pins of the Germans. Then, as the Polish Army collapsed, the red-topped pins were swept off the maps and dropped into a box.

These were Germany's days of glory, the days when the black-topped pins everywhere moved forward invincibly. Five years later, these same pins were dropped one by one into another box signalling defeat, absolute and utter, on all fronts, in the air, at sea and in the rubble of its ancient cities.

Churchill, who was a man best able to appreciate a situation when it was visualized, lived with maps. After taking over as Prime Minister he had his own personal map room moved from the Admiralty to a site adjoining his own living quarters. Although the information furnished to both rooms was identical, Churchill, who hated the fluorescent tubes over the maps, preferred to look at his own versions.

Often when he was in "The Hole" and needed to pinpoint a position, he would pore over a schoolboy atlas which he kept in his desk drawer.

King George VI, who was a frequent visitor to the fortress, had no reservations about the fluorescent lighting. He liked to check not only the maps but the statistical charts with which the walls were covered.

One wall of the Map Room still carries the great sea map of the world on which fleet positions, enemy U-boats and the daily progress of convoys were charted. Here —a closely guarded secret—the whereabouts of the *Queen Mary* and the *Queen Elizabeth,* each bearing 15,000 men, were marked by special flag-topped pins.

This map, conventionally lit, was Churchill's favourite and any time he entered the Map Room he made a beeline for it. Fascinated by the movements of convoys—the lifeline of the country—he frequently asked probing questions of the men on watch as to why certain ships were not moving as rapidly as they might or why they were holed up in port.

On one particular occasion a ship caught his fancy; he learned that it was lumbering slowly through the U-boat-infested North Atlantic carrying a cargo of 6,000 tons of eggs. Daily he noted its progress, seeming to feel every pitch and roll of its passage. Finally he turned to his crony, F. E. Lindemann, the bowler-hatted Oxford don, regarded by Churchill as a sort of portable thinking machine, and asked him how many actual eggs 6,000 tons represented.

The Prof switched on the full voltage of his brainpower, considered the matter, and delivered an answer: 107 million. The Churchillian figure seemed to swell. "That means," he thundered, "two eggs for every man, woman and child in Britain!" Having solved this, the

Humour in Uniform

THEIR preliminary embarkation training over, the young marines were in the pub, swapping stories like hardened warriors. Then one of them tried to bring the Sergeant-Major into the conversation. "And how long have you been in, sir?" "Laddie," came the dour reply, "when I joined up, the Dead Sea hadn't even reported sick."

—M. A. TROTMAN, Aldeburgh, Suffolk

A GROUP of airmen were discussing the electrical appliances they planned to buy for their wives with a recent pay rise. One old timer, who had been listening with evident disgust at such extravagances, dispersed the group with the remark: "Bought my wife a clothes drier last month—200 feet of it, complete with pegs." —D. L. WOODS

ANXIOUS TO broaden our men's outlook, the Colonel arranged to give them a lecture on Keats. On the night, the Regimental Sergeant-Major took the stage to introduce the subject and the speaker. "It's come to the Colonel's notice," he began, looking around pityingly, "that some of you lot don't know what a keat is . . ."

—J. H. THOMAS, Camborne, Cornwall

ONE DAY I was explaining the several rows of ribbons on my naval uniform to an attractive young bus conductress. I purposely passed over my Long Service and Good Conduct ribbon, but she asked about it. "Oh," I replied, "that's for 15 years' good conduct."

"Good heavens!" she gasped. "Didn't you ever go ashore?"

—W. BAILEY

To ESCAPE German shellfire, I was hiding with two Australians behind a partly wrecked building. One of them, reading a book he had found, asked, "I say, what does this word mean—CATEGORY?"

"That's easy," the other Aussie said. "C-A-T spells cat, E—it is a 'e cat, and you know what GORY means. Blimey, it's a ruddy TOMCAT."

—P. HASSETT

"SERGEANT," excitedly called the sentry at the main gate. "Private Smith's just driven through!"

"So what?" bellowed the annoyed sergeant of the guard. "People drive through every day."

"But, sergeant," stammered the sentry, "the gate was *closed*."—R. E. RINER

PRE-PRINTED forms are constantly used in the U.S. Navy. But occasionally a form does not exist for a particular purpose. Recently in London I borrowed a camp bed from the Navy's Special Services Stores so that my father would be able to stay with me in my flat for a brief visit. Several days passed, and Special Services sent me this pre-printed form: "It is requested that the recreation gear that you have checked out from this office be returned."—Lieutenant L. J. BALINK, London two men were able to refocus on winning the war.

While the great egg question may have seemed trivial, it was one more proof to the Prime Minister of The Prof's giant mental resources. During the Battle of Britain and later on the road back to El Alamein, The Prof's self-confidence and Churchill's confidence in his intellect were to have a signal effect in turning Britain's effort from defensive to offensive action.

At that time, impressed by Germany's overwhelming air superiority, the military were adamant about keeping more planes in reserve than Churchill felt were necessary. Turning to The Prof for help, the Prime Minister received the answer that the military were wrong. The Prof had been studying the figures on the Map Room wall which showed the daily rate of air casualties on both sides, and had come to the conclusion, by complicated reasoning, that there were far fewer German planes than anyone had imagined. Armed with this calculation from a source he considered infallible, Churchill fought the military to a standstill and got the squadrons he wanted for his counter-attacking strategy.

After the war was over, it appeared from captured German records that The Prof had been off beam: the military were indeed right in their estimates. But in the meantime Churchill had gained his point, got his planes and prepared for the crucial battle of El Alamein.

The Very Hot Line to Washington

WHILE THE Map Room and the Cabinet Room were the heart of the operation, a small lavatory-sized room, which even has a lavatory-lock, was also a key position. Here was the scrambler telephone over which Churchill carried on his wartime conversations with President Roosevelt in the White House. The phone was installed by the U.S. Marines, and the instructions for its use, "Speak in a normal voice," are still in position on the small shelf holding the phone.

The conversations were carried on in strictest secrecy and, when the lock on the door read, "Engaged," the corridors were cleared so that no details of the transatlantic conversations could be overheard.

In the room is a clock with London time indicated by black hands and Washington time by red. Despite this, Churchill was not a man

Professor Lindemann, Churchill's scientific adviser

to be influenced by the hour if he had something on his mind. His calls were as likely to reach Washington at 3 a.m. as at a more civilized hour.

Whenever a call was made, a small comedy of manners took place. Neither Churchill nor Roosevelt relished holding the phone until the other was there and ready to speak. Consequently, once the call had been placed, Major-General Hollis or one of the secretaries held the line until he was sure the U.S. President was actually on the phone. In Washington the same procedure was followed, and the ploy of ensuring that both men came on the line at the same time had secretarial nerves snapping like banjo strings.

When Churchill finally got to the phone, he was never without a fresh cigar which he smoked throughout the conversation. The room was small and, although the edges of the door were nearly flush with the jamb, there were leaks through which the smoke could pass. As the conversation went on, smoke would come curling from the door into the corridor like wisps of smouldering brimstone from some underground entry to Hell. Then, the conversation at an end, Churchill, clad usually in his dragon-covered dressing-gown, would throw open the door and stride forth.

Describing it, one of his *aides* says, "When Winston opened the door, the sudden blaze of light in

The small room where Churchill held his "hot-line" conversations with Washington

the dark corridor, the rush of pent-up smoke, and Winston in his dragons . . . it all looked as though Lucifer had made a sudden ascent to earth and was looking for a victim—you!"

The Disappearing Chairs

"THE HOLE" came into being with a casualness as deceptive as the organization of a game of darts in a village pub.

In 1936 the Committee of Imperial Defence, following a memorandum from a cavalry colonel named Ismay, concluded that if Germany declared war on Britain, she might attack by bombing. This meant that a place must be prepared for the Cabinet and Chiefs of Staff to meet safe from bombs. The Treasury provided £500 to start the project; and two men, a Major of the Royal Marines, Leslie Hollis, and Lawrence Burgis, a civil servant from the Cabinet secretariat, were assigned to find the site.

Hollis and Burgis, after surveying the situation, decided that the best possible site would be the cellars of the building shared by the Office of Works (later renamed the Ministry of Works) and the Board of Education in Storey's Gate, within easy walking distance of No. 10 Downing Street, the Foreign Office, Buckingham Palace and Parliament. Erected in the reign of

Edward VII, the building looked solid enough to shed bombs without further strengthening. In addition, the Office of Works, who would have to be let in on the secret of the construction, had an office just over the cellars. A senior official of the Office, Eric de Normann, was taken into the confidence of Burgis and Hollis, and work got under way.

A fourth member was added to the team with the introduction of George Rance, an ex-Sergeant in the Rifle Brigade, in charge of the pay sheets of the charwomen in the Office of Works. Rance proved to be a man of vast talent and enterprise.

He was asked to clear out the old cellars and, without arousing any suspicion, fit them out with tables, chairs, lights, camp beds and a few supplies. An old soldier who knew

Lawrence Burgis and Leslie Hollis, who chose the site of This Secret Place

how to scrounge, he did the work with exemplary secrecy. One of his regular jobs was ordering furniture for the Office of Works. Now, when he was given a legitimate order for one chair he added an unauthorized order for another one, and stored the second in the cellars. He did the same with table lamps and other equipment. As time went on, he was in effect whisking van-loads of furniture to the cellars with the speed and the practised stealth of a merlin. To keep outsiders from nosing round and asking questions, special locks were fitted to the doors, and Rance held the only keys.

George Rance, "a man of talent and enterprise"

Meanwhile, maps and documents from the Admiralty, the War Office and the Foreign Office were smuggled in as well, addressed simply "c/o Mr. Rance, Office of Works, Whitehall." This became, in time, a code word for the entire operation; acts of the highest secrecy by people of the Very Highest Rank were carried out in Rance's name.

Other secret work went on under the guidance of Hollis and Burgis. The original £500 had been only enough to buy wooden beams to shore up the ceilings, but now with the help of Warren Fisher, Secretary to the Treasury, money was forthcoming to provide steel doors and air locks for barriers in case of gas attack. Soon the ceilings were festooned with the ganglia of naked electrical wiring, left exposed so that repairs could be made easily, and piping for air-conditioning. To make sure that no one realized what was going on in the cellars, the airducts were carried to another building half a mile away.

The entire operation of creating This Secret Place was tantamount to spiriting away an elephant through a crowd without anyone noticing. However, the team brought it off; throughout the war the Germans had no idea where the command post was, and remained convinced that if it existed at all, it was either under a Yorkshire moor or in the dungeons of a ruined castle.

The Least Safe Place

WHAT HAD started out to be a simple bombproof bunker had now grown into a fortress which soon required an independent water supply. Following high-level scientific discussion, a water diviner with the reputation of being able to locate a raindrop under a block of concrete was brought in. After a day of wandering round the cellars, he pointed dramatically and said, "Dig here." They dug and—Eureka!—a cascade.

This Secret Place was also equipped with specially armoured cables to supply electricity and with its own emergency generating plant. These double measures were essential, not only to keep the lights burning but to run the pumps, for the lower cellars, being at the water-level of the Thames, were in danger of flooding should a bomb score a hit.

Initially, feeding arrangements in This Secret Place merely consisted of a primitive portable stove used by the Royal Marine guards to brew up

tea. Later, after working all night it was possible to get eggs and bacon at the same source. More and more people began to rely on getting their breakfast in the cellars until finally a full-scale canteen was installed, and a dining-room for the General Staff.

The major defence for the fortress was the 15-foot-thick slab of concrete filling the space once occupied by a suite of offices just below the ground floor but above the topmost level of the cellars. Work on this went on through the Blitz, much to the annoyance of Churchill. When the sounds of workmen filtered down even into the Cabinet Room, he would halt all business and, banging his hand on the table in

The modest kitchen of the Cabinet War Rooms where staff meals were prepared

time to his prose, roar at one of the secretaries, "Can you not stop that damned knock, knock, KNOCKING?"

After one of these outbursts the noise would stop, but in time it led to a sort of game between the workmen and Churchill. Daily, word was passed via Rance as to Churchill's whereabouts. If he was in the building, not a workman stirred; if he was not, work went on at top speed. But Churchill's movements were unpredictable, and the men took to doing their job with one eye on a lookout who warned them when to bang and when to retire for a cup of tea.

Despite the interruptions, the slab, reinforced with a criss-cross of old tram lines, was finally finished and calculated to be solid enough to withstand the force of a 500-pound bomb. To give further protection, wire-netting was woven round the airshafts and stair well.

One night during the Blitz when a 1,000-pounder fell within 50 yards, Churchill grumbled because it wasn't closer. "Help us to test our defences," he growled.

It was perhaps fortunate he never got his wish, for "The Hole's" resistance to damage was more theoretical than practical. After the war, Lawrence Burgis said, "We didn't know how unsafe we really were. True, a direct hit wouldn't have caused us any harm, but if a bomb had come in at an angle it would have demolished us. The

engineers told us later that under air attack, the fortress was one of the least safe places in London."

The Famous "V"

WHEN A chance hit from a German bomb demolished part of No. 10 Downing Street, Churchill and his family moved to a flat prepared for them in a suite of offices immediately over the cellars. This was known as the Annexe and its defence from bombs consisted almost entirely of steel shutters fitted to the windows.

In theory, Churchill and his family were to retire to their quarters in "The Hole" itself when the bombing grew intense. But although Churchill did have the bed-sitting room there, he merely used the bed to lounge on like a cherubic, cigar-smoking Madame Récamier while he carried on discussions with his ministers who sat in chairs surrounding him.

One night during severe bombing an *aide* insisted that he go down to the underground bedroom, in deference to Mrs. Churchill's wishes. Churchill in bad grace acquiesced, bundling up his papers and shuffling downstairs in his slippers. He undressed, got into bed, remained for a minute. Then he got up again, took his papers and began making his way upstairs. The *aide* remonstrated but Churchill silenced him with "I agreed to go downstairs to the bedroom . . . I have *been* downstairs to the bedroom. I am now

Winston Churchill and his wife Clementine inspecting bomb damage during the Blitz

going upstairs to work and later to sleep. We have both kept our words."

But for Churchill to remain indoors under any circumstances during the nights of the Blitz was unusual. Artfully dodging an almost direct order from the King, as well as the entreaties of his staff, he insisted not only on watching the raids but on appearing as quickly as possible anywhere bombs had fallen.

It was during his night-bombing appearances that Churchill began to use his V-for-Victory sign—a symbol inspired by a scene which took place during the Battle of Britain. As reports of the failure of the last great thrust of the Luftwaffe came into the Map Room, a young officer cut out four strips of paper which he pasted round the V of the royal cypher for "Victoria Regina" marked on the face of the clock. Churchill, coming into the room to learn the score of the downed planes, noted the framed "V." For several minutes he stood looking at it in silence, then turned abruptly and left.

Thereafter, the mark which had been born in the Map Room reappeared in the bombed streets of London and across the world, in Churchill's upraised right hand—a sign of confidence and hope.

"We Have Made History"

ALSO IN Churchill's underground bed-sitting room is his desk, a continent-sized cube of well-worn mahogany, where he signed State papers and wrote his memoranda. There are still unused envelopes in a small stationery holder on the desk, a blunted pencil and two candlesticks.

It was at this desk that Churchill made four of his most important broadcasts. The first was on May 19, 1940, when, with the armies of France in broken disarray, he warned in rolling sentences of a battle to come—the battle for Britain. "Arm yourselves," he quoted, "and be ye men of valour!"

A month later, as Britain tensed for the blow which Hitler stood ready to launch from the air, Churchill stated the situation's gravity and then in one sentence summed up the spirit of all resistance to tyranny, everywhere: "Let us therefore brace ourselves to our duties, and so bear ourselves that, if the British Empire and its Commonwealth last for a thousand years, men will still say: *'This* was their finest hour!'"

That hour, if one can be pinpointed, came soon after—on September 15, 1940. That was when, after being pounded by the RAF, the Luftwaffe turned tail and fled.

On October 21, 1940, when the Battle of Britain was almost over, Churchill spoke from the bedroom a third time, this time to the stricken French. There was no chair in the room for the announcer, and the microphone could not be moved. So Michel Saint-Denis had to introduce the Prime Minister while sitting on his knee. Then Churchill spoke, in such French as can only be spoken by an Englishman. Quoting Napoleon he said, "These same Prussians who are so boastful today were three to one at Jena and six to one at Montmirail. Never," he went on, "will I believe that the soul of France is dead. *Vive la France!*"

"After he had finished," recalls Saint-Denis, "there was a silence. We were all deeply stirred. Then Churchill stood. 'We have made history tonight,' he said, and his eyes were full of tears."

As the duel between Britain and

Winston Churchill's desk

Germany moved into its second year, conditions had changed perceptibly and it was no longer quite so one-sided.

A supremely confident Churchill went on the air again on February 9, 1941. Ignoring the fact that the odds were still against victory, he said to the American people and their leader, "Give us the tools, and we will finish the job."

A recent visitor to This Secret Place looked at the desk and, as the guide told the story of the four speeches, said, "All my life I have heard that when danger threatened Drake's Drum would beat. But I never thought it could take the form of a human voice from behind a desk."

The P.M. and the Sergeant-Major

IF IT was the personality of Churchill that gave This Secret Place its character, it was the skill of George Rance that kept things running smoothly. The relationship between the two men was a delicately poised one. Both were old soldiers. Both were the same age: Churchill had taken power on Rance's birthday, and this, Rance felt, had a special significance.

Of course one was the Prime Minister and the other the custodian, but it was more a feeling of the Colonel of the Regiment and the Regimental Sergeant-Major. If the "Old Boss," as everyone referred to him, wanted Rance to do something that Rance felt was out of order, Rance did not hesitate to say so.

Once Churchill decided that his bed faced the wrong way. Rance replied that it was all right for the Prime Minister to want to have his bed shifted, but the fact remained that there were two beams which prevented the shift. Churchill looked at the bed, at Rance, and at the beams and slammed out of the room. Later word was passed to Rance that the P.M. knew that he had acted correctly and it would be perfectly all right if they both forgot the entire thing.

Although Churchill specialized in demanding the seemingly impossible, he asked it only of those people he knew and whom he felt were not extending their capabilities to their fullest stretch. They might be generals reluctant to risk defeat, admirals wary of losing their ships, politicians fearful of harming their careers or ex-Sergeant George Rance.

After the first meeting in the Cabinet Room, Churchill called Rance for a private word. "Those chairs are no good," he said. "Their seats are too hard. I want new ones by tonight."

"It can't be done," Rance answered.

"I *want* it done," Churchill thundered back.

Rance could scarcely restrain himself from stamping his foot, saluting and saying "Saah!"

Calling the Office of Works to report that he needed 24 new chairs delivered at the double, Rance was informed that it wasn't possible. "I will now tell you what the Prime Minister told me," Rance said, and told them.

The chairs were delivered and in place for the Cabinet meeting.

A devourer of information, Churchill was also a lover of brevity on the part of others. At Cabinet meetings if a subject was of interest to him, he would ask for an immediate report dealing in minute detail with every aspect of the problem—all on not more than one sheet of paper. To satisfy this, a typewriter was located whose type was almost small enough to record the wisdom of Confucius on a grain of rice.

At the same time, when reading his own speeches Churchill demanded a type so large that a long Churchillian sentence, complete with drum-rolls, barely went on to one page. This, too, was supplied by Rance.

Mrs. Churchill also relied on Rance. She too had an underground room—separated by only a thin door from the bed-sitting room where Churchill and his colleagues habitually stayed up, thrashing out the war's problems.

Finally Mrs. Churchill called for Rance. "My husband goes on talking all night long," she said. "Can't you do something to reduce the noise?"

Rance considered the situation—and finally managed to block off the

The "Old Boss," as Churchill became known

door with a thick layer of baize. From that time on, the Prime Minister, wreathed in cigar smoke, talked through the night, and while bombs fell Mrs. Churchill and Mary Churchill—who had a camp bed in the same room when off duty from her anti-aircraft unit—slept undisturbed.

But usually Mrs. Churchill's requests were aimed at giving her husband what small comforts could be found in wartime.

On one occasion, when Churchill was due to return from a journey, Rance was asked by Mrs. Churchill to think up a small surprise. Someone had sent the Old Boss a small black wooden cat as a mascot. Rance made a small wooden wall for the cat to peer over. Churchill was delighted with the gift and put it on his bedside table.

On the way back to his office Rance met an august admiral who asked, "How is the Prime Minister?"

"Very well, sir," Rance replied. "When I left him, he was playing with his toy cat."

When invasion seemed imminent, preparations were made to resist should This Secret Place be attacked. Above ground, the Home Guard manned a pillbox at the corner of the building, and just inside the door were a group of Grenadier Guards, named Rance's Guard for security reasons—the only time a private person has been so singled out in the Regiment's 300-year history. Below, inside the fortress itself, were men of the Royal Marines.

Fitted to the walls were rifle racks. If the attack had come, these guns would have been passed out to help hold the fortress to the last man. The Old Boss himself had his service revolver from the First World War, and in his desk was a dagger.

When George VI paid a visit during the darkest days of the war, he noticed the dagger and asked its purpose. "For Mr. Churchill, sir," Rance replied. "So that he can use it when Hitler is brought before him." Mr. Churchill listened but did not add anything to the statement.

Although the pressure was intense, the undercurrent of impish waggery which the Old Boss seemed to inspire never vanished from This Secret Place.

Ernest Bevin, Minister of Labour

Since the moles, as the inmates called themselves, lived almost entirely underground—the principal Cabinet Ministers all had small bedrooms, and the staff were furnished with dormitories—the weather on the surface was an unknown quantity. To provide this information, Rance had made a board with movable strips. These were labelled *Rain, Snow, Sunny* and on through all the permutations of English weather, which were changed as reports were phoned below. Another board showed if London was under air attack or not.

Puckishly Ernie Bevin would invariably change the weather board signal to *Windy* when bombing was reported. One day a young officer beat Bevin to the draw by posting in the weather slot a sign from a pub saying *No Gin*.

Bevin prepared to make the habitual change to *Windy,* noted the *No Gin* sign. "Gawd 'elp us," he muttered, "it's worse than windy." He let the sign stand.

"A Flaming Maharaja"

EARLY IN the war Sir Archibald Sinclair, the Secretary of State for Air, had told Churchill about one of his men who had been on duty a long time without leave and had then collapsed when he finally got home. "Serves him right for going on leave," the Old Boss answered. In 1943 after the danger of invasion was past and Britain was on the offensive, the pressures caught up with even the indomitable Churchill himself. After a trip to Africa, he caught pneumonia and word was passed that "the Old Boss was laid up."

Immobilized in bed, he sent for Rance. The ex-Sergeant was shaken when he saw how pale the Prime Minister looked, and no hint of a cigar anywhere. His voice was feeble but his words, although slurred, were plain.

Aerial view of the Storey's Gate building, with Big Ben in the background

He was sure that some of the pictures in his room were not hanging properly. Would Rance adjust them?

Rance looked round the room. Portraits of Churchill's parents hung on the walls, a small shelf Rance had made to hold some of his trinkets was in place, the black cat peering over the wall was on the bedside table.

He saw the picture the Old Boss meant. As he began to shift it, Churchill's voice seemed to grow stronger, indicating the direction the picture ought to be moved. Finally he was satisfied—and in fact when Rance turned round, Churchill was sitting up in bed, the ghost of his old-time spark beginning to

glitter in his eyes. "Not quite gone yet," he said. "Eyes just as good as ever."

This time Rance did say "Saah," although when he stamped his foot it was very softly.

But after a second bout of pneumonia Churchill's legs could no longer manage the stairs. He continued to attend Cabinet meetings in "The Hole," but came downstairs in a sort of sedan chair carried by two Royal Marines. "Looks like a flaming maharaja, don't he?" said one of the guards. Rance, who remembered him racing through the corridors, trailed by a nimbus of admirals and generals, could only nod.

In This Secret Place the war had begun with Ismay glancing at his watch and saying, at 11 a.m. on September 3, 1939, "Gentlemen, we are at war with Germany."

It ended just as casually when, on August 16, 1945, the phones stopped ringing and one by one the officers left their desks.

George Rance turned out the lights in their offices, closed the doors, and climbed the stairs into the sunshine. That was the end—almost.

On January 30, 1965, the long, slow cortège of the funeral of Sir Winston Spencer Churchill wound through London—from Westminster to the City. The scars of the war had now been long obliterated. There was nothing to mark the block which had hidden the wartime fortress, only a blank brick wall.

In St. Paul's Cathedral George Rance, now 91 years old, sat in a back pew and watched. He remembered then the few gruff words that had passed between the ex-Lieutenant-Colonel of the Royal Scots Fusiliers and the ex-Sergeant of the Rifle Brigade, when the war was over. "I suppose, Rance," Churchill had said, "you think I don't know all you have done. Well, I do. Thank you. Thank you very much." THE END

VE Day, 1945, celebrating a victory masterminded in "This Secret Place"

A Reader's Digest "First Person" Award

My Ride on a Torpedo

By Vice-Admiral Harry DeWolf, C.B.E., D.S.O., D.S.C.
Chief of Staff, Royal Canadian Navy (Retd.)

W HEN I retired after 40-odd years in the Royal Canadian Navy, a reporter commenting on my service career wrote that I had once ridden a torpedo like a cowboy around the deck of a destroyer. The story arose from an incident aboard the Canadian destroyer *St. Laurent.* I was her captain, with the rank of lieutenant-commander.

On July 1, 1940, *St. Laurent,* with three British destroyers, was escorting the battleship H.M.S. *Nelson* towards the United Kingdom. That day, as was customary in both the British and Canadian navies, the semiannual promotion list was broadcast. I was promoted to commander and ordered to report at Halifax, Nova Scotia, for new assignment. My relief was to be Lieutenant-Commander Herbert Rayner, a torpedo specialist. In the busy week that followed, the men of our torpedo department had no time to spruce up their weapons for their

newcoming skipper's inspection. And who could suspect that when they did one lad in an excess of zeal would let loose a torpedo against the ship itself?

Early on July 2, *St. Laurent* was detached on a successful search for survivors from a liner torpedoed that morning west of Ireland. We landed 859 survivors at Greenock, on the west coast of Scotland, and were then ordered to Rosyth, a naval base on the east coast.

On a fine Sunday afternoon, in company with another Canadian destroyer, H.M.C.S. *Skeena,* we were steaming up the west coast en route to Rosyth by way of the Minches and Pentland Firth. *Skeena* followed on our starboard quarter, about 300 yards away. Sailing north inside the Western Isles, in somewhat protected waters, we were relatively safe from the enemy.

The torpedomen on watch were cleaning, polishing and painting the torpedo tubes. All tubes were loaded, but they had safety devices to prevent accidental firing, one being a simple hand-operated latch.

A battery of four tubes is normally trained fore and aft, and is pivoted outboard before a torpedo is aimed and fired. An explosive charge then catapults the greased, 24-foot-long, ton-and-a-half steel "fish" out of its tube and safely clear of the launching ship's side. The torpedo's engine starts as the missile makes this leap.

At the tail two counter-rotating propellers, powered by fuel and compressed air at 200 atmospheres of pressure, drive the deadly thing towards its target at speeds up to 45 knots. As the nose courses through the water, its dormant 600-pound warhead of TNT is alerted by a device called a "pistol." The rushing sea water spins a four-bladed propeller down a threaded stem inside the nose to unwind a safety device. Now the torpedo is armed and will explode at the slightest contact with any of the four blades.

It was on such a carefully designed infernal machine, at 18.05 hours that July afternoon, that a young seaman-torpedoman, intent only on his painting and finding the firing lever in his way, lifted the safety catch and pulled back the firing lever. The lad's brush never reached its mark. With an explosive *WHOOMP!* the torpedo leaped free.

I was in my sea cabin on the starboard side of the bridge when I was aroused by a terrific clatter. I rushed out, looked aft, and was greeted by an unusual sight. A torpedo was loose on the steel deck, and its propellers were beating a noisy tattoo as it bumped along.

Since the torpedo had been fired towards the stern, its first rush down the deck tore loose some heavy ammunition boxes and carried away the starboard ladder (a substantial, rigidly mounted, plated-steel staircase). It mounted the three-inch-gun platform to butt an anti-aircraft gun a glancing blow, then crashed into the after superstructure head on. From there it rebounded to the starboard side of the deck. When I first sighted the frenzied machine from the bridge, it was charging the superstructure for the second time. It had not yet become armed—but it might at any moment.

A glance showed me *Skeena* off our starboard quarter. I ordered a message: I HAVE A TORPEDO LOOSE ON MY STARBOARD DECK. *Skeena* immediately shifted over smartly to our port quarter, keeping on the lee side of *St. Laurent* and its problem. She might well be needed by survivors.

I made for the scene of action astern, although I had no idea what I might do when I got there. Fortunately, the torpedo gunner's mate, Chief Petty Officer Sam Ridge, a man who did know what to do, arrived at the same time. *St. Laurent* had only a gentle roll on, or we could have done nothing. The torpedo, its propeller blades clawing madly for purchase on the overlapping, riveted-steel deck plates, was rolling with each motion of the ship. It would lurch forward with each heave of the deck; then, as the deck came level, the torpedo would stop, like a bull in the ring, undecided in which direction to make its next charge. When it rolled against the guardrails, we advanced and held it there momentarily by bracing our legs against its flank and holding on to the top guardrail. Ridge ran to get a key to turn off

the compressed air that was driving the propellers.

St. Laurent's next roll was sufficient to make the torpedo roll away from the guardrail. At this point, I straddled it, and grabbed hold of the guardrail. The deadly 24-foot cylinder, though only 21 inches in diameter, seemed broader than a horse's back to me. It was covered with a preservative grease, and as slippery as the greased pole we boys used to try to ride during summer regattas back home in Nova Scotia.

Now I could feel the propeller blades rattling on the steel deck start to drive it forward. As the torpedo advanced, I resisted as much as I could, while going forward hand over hand along the guardrail with my legs locked on the cylinder. Unless I kept my place astride, the propellers could make mincemeat of one end of me—and free the mechanical beast to blow up a good destroyer. These antics, no doubt, led to the story of "riding the torpedo."

After Ridge returned with the key, he and the torpedo gunner, R. L. Ellis, who had arrived at the scene, were able to wrestle the torpedo steady until we could turn off the air. Once the noise of the propellers was stopped, the situation became a bit less tense, more help arrived, and the torpedo was securely lashed against the guardrails.

Now the curious began to gather. The crash against the after deckhouse had pushed the torpedo's pistol back into the warhead, and so damaged the whole front end that it could not be safely touched. We were able to remove the warhead from the torpedo, but even so the warhead and its pistol remained a touchy problem, a quarter of a ton of sensitive explosive.

There was no help readily available at the dockside when we arrived in Rosyth next day. I went straight to local headquarters to report for orders and also to note that I had a damaged torpedo and wanted a replacement. I received instructions to sail at once with a convoy to its dispersal point in the North Atlantic. My torpedo problem, I was told, would be taken care of by another department!

When I returned to the ship, I found that my crew had managed to hoist the torpedo and the damaged warhead on to the jetty without dockyard help. I reported by signal, briefly, how the torpedo had been damaged and where it had been left, and so to sea.

On my return to the United Kingdom—fortunately not to Rosyth, but to Liverpool—I was met by Lieutenant-Commander Rayner, who took over the ship. I was safely back in Canada by the time the very angry Rosyth dockyard authorities caught up with *St. Laurent,* which had left them holding such an awkward baby.

I had in the meantime written a full report of the incident to Commander-in-Chief, Western Approaches. In this report I suggested that a court of inquiry would be unnecessary, because there was nothing to be learned. The young torpedoman freely admitted what he had done and that was that.

The Rosyth dockyard was understandably put out, because nobody wanted to touch the damaged warhead, let alone move it. Lieutenant-Commander Rayner was able to fend off their furious enquiries by referring to my written report, which answered everything except what to do with the remains. In the end, we learned, they secured it to a ground mine, and laid it in a North Sea minefield.

A Reader's Digest "First Person" Award

The Unexpected Armistice

By Fritz Vincken

WHEN we heard the knock on our door that Christmas Eve in 1944, neither Mother nor I had the slightest inkling of the quiet miracle that lay in store for us.

I was 12 then, and we were living in a small cottage in the Ardennes, near the German-Belgian border. Father had stayed at the cottage for hunting week-ends before the war, but when Allied bombers reduced our home town of Aachen to rubble, he sent us to live there. He had been ordered into the civil defence fire guard in the border town of Monschau, four miles away.

"You'll be safe in the woods," he had told me. "Take care of Mother. You're the man of the family now."

But a week earlier Field-Marshal von Rundstedt

had launched the last, desperate German offensive of the war and now, as I went to the door, the Battle of the Bulge was raging all around us. We heard the incessant booming of field guns; planes roared continuously overhead; and at night searchlights stabbed through the darkness. Thousands of Allied and German soldiers were fighting and dying near by.

Steel Helmets. When the first knock came, Mother blew out the candles; then, as I went to the door, she stepped ahead of me and pushed it open. Outside, like ghosts against the snow-clad trees, stood two steel-helmeted men. One of them spoke to mother in a language we did not understand, pointing to a third man, lying in the snow. She realized before I did that these were American soldiers. *Enemies!*

Mother stood silent, motionless, her hand on my shoulder. They were armed and could have forced their way in, yet they stood there and asked with their eyes. The wounded man seemed more dead than alive. *"Komm' rein,"* Mother said at last. The soldiers carried their comrade inside and laid him on my bed.

None of them understood German. But Mother tried French and found that one of the soldiers could converse haltingly with her. As she went to look after the wounded man, she said to me, "The fingers of those two are numb. Take off their jackets and boots and bring in

a bucket of snow." Soon I was rubbing their blue feet with snow.

We learned that the stocky, dark-haired fellow was Jim; his friend, tall and slender, was Robin. Harry, the wounded one, was now sleeping on my bed, his face as white as the snow outside. They'd lost their battalion and had wandered through the forest for three days, looking for the Americans, hiding from the Germans. They hadn't shaved but, without their heavy coats, they still looked like boys. And that was just how Mother began to treat them.

"Go and get Hermann," she said to me, "and bring six potatoes."

This was a serious departure from our pre-Christmas plans. Hermann was our plump rooster (named after Hermann Goering, for whom Mother had little affection). We'd been fattening him up for weeks in the hope that Father would be home for Christmas. But some hours before, when it was obvious he would not make it, Mother decreed that Hermann should live for a few more days, in case Father could get home for New Year's Eve. Now she had changed her mind again—Hermann would serve an immediate, pressing purpose.

While Jim and I helped with the cooking, Robin took care of Harry, who had been shot in the thigh, and almost bled to death. Mother tore a sheet into long strips for bandages.

Soon, the tempting smell of roast chicken permeated our room. I was laying the table when once again there came a knock on the door. Expecting to find more lost Americans, I opened it without hesitation. There stood four soldiers, wearing uniforms quite familiar to me after five years of war. They were *Wehrmacht*—our own!

More Guests. I was paralysed with fear. Although a child, I knew the law: sheltering enemy soldiers constituted high treason. We could all be shot! Mother was frightened, too. Her face was white, but she stepped outside and said quietly, *"Fröhliche Weihnachten."* The soldiers wished her a Merry Christmas, too.

"We have lost our regiment and would like to wait for daylight," explained the corporal. "Can we rest here?"

"Of course," Mother replied, with a calmness born of panic. "You can also have a good warm meal and eat till the pot is empty."

The Germans smiled as they sniffed the aroma through the half-open door. "But," Mother added firmly, "we have three other guests, whom you may not consider friends." Now her voice was suddenly sterner than I'd ever heard it before.

"This is Christmas Eve, and there will be no shooting here."

"Who's inside?" the corporal demanded. "Americans?"

Mother looked at each frost-chilled face. "Listen," she said slowly. "You could be my sons, and so could those in there. A boy with

a gunshot wound, fighting for his life. His two friends—lost, and just as hungry and exhausted as you are. This one night," she turned to the corporal and raised her voice a little, "this Christmas night, let us forget about killing."

The corporal stared at her. There were several endless seconds of silence. Then Mother put an end to indecision. "Enough talking!" she ordered and clapped her hands sharply. "Please put your weapons here on the wood-pile—and hurry up before the others eat all the dinner!"

Obediently, the four soldiers placed their arms on the pile of firewood just inside the door: two pistols, three carbines, a light machine-gun and two bazookas. Meanwhile, Mother was speaking French rapidly to Jim. He said something in English, and to my amazement I saw the American boys, too, turn their weapons over to Mother.

Now, as Germans and Americans tensely rubbed elbows in the small room, Mother was really on her mettle. Never losing her smile, she tried to find a seat for everyone. We had only three chairs, but Mother's bed was big, and on it she placed two of the newcomers side by side with Jim and Robin.

Impervious to the strained atmosphere, Mother went on preparing dinner. But Hermann wasn't going to grow any bigger, and there were four more mouths to feed. "Quick," she whispered to me, "get more potatoes and some oats. These boys are hungry, and a starving man is an angry one."

While foraging in the larder, I heard Harry moan. When I returned, one of the Germans had put on his glasses to inspect the American's wound.

"Do you belong to the Medical Corps?" Mother asked him.

"No," he replied, "but I studied medicine at Heidelberg until a few months ago." Thanks to the cold, he told the Americans in what sounded like fairly good English, Harry's wound hadn't become infected. "He is suffering from severe loss of blood," he explained to Mother. "What he needs is rest and nourishment."

Relaxation was now beginning to replace suspicion. Even to me, all the soldiers looked very young as we sat there together. Heinz and Willi, both from Cologne, were 16. The German corporal, at 23, was the oldest of them all. From his food bag he provided a bottle of red wine, and Heinz managed to find a loaf of

rye bread. Mother cut it in small pieces to be served with the dinner; half the wine, however, she put away. "For the wounded boy."

Then Mother said grace. I noticed that there were tears in her eyes as she said the old, familiar words, *"Komm, Herr Jesus. Be our guest."* And as I looked round the table, I saw tears, too, in the eyes of the battle-weary soldiers, boys again, some from America, some from Germany, all far from home.

Just before midnight, Mother went to the doorstep and asked us to join her and look up at the Star of Bethlehem. We all stood beside her except Harry, who was blissfully sleeping. For all of us during that moment of silence, looking at Sirius, the brightest star in the heavens, the war was a very distant, almost forgotten thing.

"Be Careful." Our private armistice continued next morning. Harry woke in the early hours, mumbling in his drowsiness, then swallowed some broth that Mother fed to him. With the dawn, it was apparent that he was becoming stronger. Mother made him an invigorating drink from our one egg, the rest of the corporal's wine and some sugar. Everyone else had oatmeal. Afterwards, two poles and Mother's best tablecloth were fashioned into a stretcher for Harry.

The corporal then advised the Americans how to find their way back to their lines. (At that stage of the fluid battle, the Germans were surprisingly well-informed.) Looking at Jim's map, the corporal pointed out a stream.

"Continue along this," he said, "and you will find the First Army rebuilding its forces on its upper course."

"Why not at Monschau?" Jim asked. *"Um Himmels Willen!*

Nein!" the corporal exclaimed. "We've retaken Monschau."

Now mother gave them all back their weapons. "Be careful, boys," she said. "I want you to get home some day where you belong. God bless you all!" The German and American soldiers shook hands, and we watched them disappear in opposite directions.

When I went back inside, Mother had brought out the old family Bible. I glanced over her shoulder. The book was open at the Christmas story, telling of the Birth in the Manger and how the Wise Men came from afar bearing their gifts. Her finger was tracing the last line *". . . they departed into their own country another way."*

Poetic Licence

WHEN Robert Frost was asked to explain one of his poems, he replied, "What do you want me to do—say it over again in worser English?"

—H. E. F. Donohue

*   *   *

The Age of Discretion

ZSA ZSA GABOR tells about the time her daughter, then 15, asked, "Mummy, how old are you?" Replied Zsa Zsa, "I'm 21, darling." Thoughtful pause, then : "Mummy, I have a feeling that some day I may be older than you."

—M. B.

NOEL COWARD once remarked of Gloria Swanson, who stays incredibly young-looking : "She looks like an old, old 12."

—R. H.

JAMES DENTON, a publicity director of Twentieth Century Fox studios, was asked how he obtained the ages of his contract screen actresses. "We use the half-and-half method," he explained. "The exact age of any woman is obtained by adding half the years she acknowledges to half the years her best friend gives her."

—*Parade*

Humour in Uniform

An N.C.O., having a tough time shaping up a batch of recruits, finally shouted, "Close up, men, close up! If the enemy were to fire on you when you're straggling along like that, they couldn't hit a damn one of you! Close up!" —R. S. K.

The shy young bride of a new lieutenant was making an overdue courtesy call on the wife of the camp's commanding officer. "It's simple," her husband had told her reassuringly. "When the maid answers the door, just ask her if the general's wife is receiving."

But when the door was answered, not by a maid but by the general himself, the young wife was thrown into confusion. Blushing furiously, she blurted, "I just dropped in to see if your wife is expecting." —Harold Coffin

On a visit to a U.S. Air Force missile base, a group of businessmen were being taken through one of the many impressive technical departments. Computers and "memory" banks were humming and ticking; maps, charts and graphs lined the walls.

Stopping before a map which depicted the local area, a visitor asked a technician the significance of the numerous coloured pins.

"Those gold pins show the location of fighter units on stand-by," the young man explained. "The green ones pinpoint missile sites under construction."

Obviously impressed, the civilian asked, "And what do these yellow pins indicate?"

The technician reddened, stuttered, and finally blurted out, "Well, sir, the yellow pins indicate the locations of the best fishing spots." —John Drew

After long years of peace, the Indian Army was jolted out of its easy-going ways by the Munich crisis of 1938. Among other things, all units were ordered to revise the detailed plans necessary to get them on a war footing. That this was somewhat overdue was emphasized by the section dealing with officers. This section opened with the statement: "On receipt of mobilization orders, officers will sharpen swords." —L. H. Packard

It was well known that the day after a big party our company commander signed his correspondence and requests without reading them. Taking advantage of this, an enterprising soldier applied for two days' extra leave. Reason: "None." He promptly got it back, approved. But on his return the staff sergeant served him with papers for two weeks' confinement to barracks. Reason: "None." —K. E.

I SHOT
DOWN YAMAMOTO

By Thomas Lanphier

That day at Arlington Cemetery was raw and rainy; a cold wind tugged at the American flag that draped my brother's coffin. With me at the graveside were my father and mother, and my other brother Jim. The war had ended four years ago, but the body of my quiet, brave young brother Charles had only just been returned to Washington from the South Pacific. As I listened to the sad, solemn words of the chaplain, I thought of how strangely my brother's life and mine had been linked with Bougainville, a remote island in the Solomons, and with a man neither of us ever saw — Admiral Isoroku Yamamoto,

commander-in-chief of the Japanese navy.

When Pearl Harbour plunged the United States into war it was almost inevitable that Charlie and I should become pilots, for our father had been a pioneer army air officer in the First World War. Charlie was still training when I was sent to Guadalcanal—the largest of the Solomon Islands—with an Army P-38 fighter squadron. Then, one March day in 1943 as I was returning from a combat patrol, I heard a familiar voice on the radio. It was Charlie! He, too, was flying over Guadalcanal, returning from a mission.

During the following weeks our paths crossed frequently. On one occasion we even tangled with the same flight of enemy Zeros; and once I helped rescue him when he had to bale out over Japanese-held territory.

Late on the afternoon of April 17, 1943, I was ordered to report to our operations dug-out. I arrived with Major John Mitchell, commanding officer of our squadron and the leading ace on Guadalcanal. As we entered the musty dug-out we saw instantly that something big was on. Most of the top brass on the island were there. Face tense, a marine major handed us a document marked Top Secret.

This told us that Yamamoto and

his senior staff officers were arriving at Bougainville by air on April 18. "Squadron 339 P-38 must at all costs reach and destroy," the dispatch said. "President attaches extreme importance this operation." It went on to say that Yamamoto and his staff would be flying in two bombers escorted by six Zeros, and then gave a detailed schedule of the flight.

Target. No wonder there was tension. Yamamoto was not only chief of the Japanese navy; he was the architect of the sneak attack on Pearl Harbour that had crippled the U.S. Pacific fleet and taken some 2,000 lives! Mitchell and I looked at each other. Bougainville was 300 miles away. Our Lockheed Lightnings were the only planes on Guadalcanal with enough range to intercept the Admiral.

Yamamoto, then 59, was a stocky, poker-faced officer who had built up the modern Japanese navy, and perfected the night-fighting and torpedo techniques which took such a terrible toll of American ships. A pioneer aviator, he helped develop the deadly Zero, and his reliance on the aircraft carrier had done much to revolutionize naval warfare.

Ironically, Yamamoto was a staunch admirer of America. He had been a brilliant student at Harvard University, a popular naval attaché in Washington. He spoke fluent English, loved poker and baseball. In fact, some authorities in Japan considered him so pro-American that he was once threatened with

assassination. Yet when the army forced Japan into war against the United States, Yamamoto directed the navy with characteristic skill and dedication.

The decision to attack his plane was not taken lightly. The opportunity came as a result of one of the biggest secrets of the war—the fact that U.S. cryptographers had broken the Japanese code, enabling us to decipher the enemy's secret messages. When it was learned that Yamamoto would come within striking distance, President Roosevelt was consulted. Was this warfare or murder? Did Japan have anyone to take his place?

The consensus was, it did not. Since Yamamoto was a vital element in the enemy's war effort, he must be eliminated.

In our dug-out, a lively argument broke out as to the best means of doing the job. Yamamoto was due at the big Kahili airstrip on Bougainville at 9.45 the next morning; we finally determined to intercept him in flight ten minutes earlier, at a point 35 miles north of there. It was a long shot. We had only 18 planes for the mission, while the Japanese had more than 100 at Kahili. And even with extra tanks, our planes could not carry enough fuel to tarry over the target area. The mission would require clock-like precision to have even the remotest chance of success.

Later, Major Mitchell briefed our group. "Take-off will be at 0725," he said. "My section of 14 planes will be at 20,000 feet to take care of the fighters from Kahili. Lanphier's section of four planes will be at 10,000 feet to make the interception."

An army intelligence officer told us how important Yamamoto was to the Japanese navy, and what a blow to enemy morale his loss would be.

"He's a perfectionist," the officer added. "Our intelligence stresses his promptness. You must be on the dot."

Sunday, April 18, broke clear but humid on Guadalcanal. As I taxied over the muddy steel matting of the runway, I got a wave and a grin from my wing man, Lieutenant Rex Barber.

At exactly 7.25, Mitchell roared down the runway and into the sky. Barber and I followed. But misfortune struck the other two planes in my group. One blew a tyre on the runway and the second one's belly tanks were not functioning properly. The mission was only minutes old and already we had lost two planes.

Mitchell waved two of his planes over to join me. Then we all headed north, flying just above the waves to escape detection by Japanese radar.

As we roared along under the blazing mid-morning sun, our 16 tightly-grouped Lightnings maintained strict radio silence. For most of two hours we were out of sight of land. I had the usual pre-combat

butterflies. I had learned from almost 100 combat missions that there are degrees of courage; on some days a pilot is more willing to risk his life than on others. But this time I felt we were all determined to risk everything.

At last Bougainville loomed ahead, a big island whose matted jungle grew right down to the water's edge. As we crossed the coastline Mitchell put his plane into a steep climb, leading his section up to 20,000 feet. My group was right behind, climbing to 10,000 feet. I glanced at my dashboard clock—9.33 a.m. Two minutes to go.

As we climbed I scanned the immensity of sky, saw nothing but a few cumulus clouds. Any minute we would surely be spotted by Japanese planes flying in and out of Kahili. Where was the punctual Admiral?

On Schedule! A moment later a pilot broke radio silence—"Bogeys. Ten o'clock high," he said quietly. Sure enough, in the distance was a V formation of dark specks. As they came nearer I saw two green-camouflaged, twin-engine bombers, escorted by six Zeros. It was 9.35—the Admiral was right on schedule! And so were we. The concerted effort of a multitude of people had brought us to this exact spot in the vast Pacific sky at the exact moment. Now it was up to us.

I prepared to attack. Ahead and above, the Japanese formation flew towards us, still oblivious of our presence.

Suddenly our luck took a turn for the worse: one of the pilots in my group was having trouble with his plane and had to turn off down the coast; his wing man had no choice but to go with him. Now Barber and I would have to do the job alone.

Combat. We were about a mile in front of the Japanese and closing fast when the Zeros spotted us. They nosed over to head us off, the lead bomber plunging towards the jungle while the second zoomed directly at us. As I dived at the first bomber three more Zeros came for me. I brought my guns to bear on the leader. We almost collided head on before the stream of bullets from my guns ripped one of his wings away. He twisted under me, trailing flame and smoke.

At that moment, in an almost vertical climb, I put my plane over on its back and looked for the bomber I had lost in the mêlée.

Sheer panic does wonders for the vision. In one glance I saw Barber tangling with some Zeros even as two others came at me. Then I saw a green shadow streaking across the jungle below—the bomber, skimming just over the trees. I followed it down to tree-top level, and began firing. Its right engine and right wing began to burn. Then the wing fell off, and the bomber crashed in the jungle.

By this time, Barber had shot down the other Japanese bomber in the ocean. It was time we made for home—fast.

I zig-zagged over the jungle, trying to shake the Zeros off my tail. Suddenly I was blinded by dust—unwittingly I had flown over one corner of the Kahili airfield. The dust was being kicked up by swarms of Japanese fighters scrambling into the air. I pressed on, across the harbour and out over the sea. Then I put my Lightning into the speed climb for which it was built and gradually pulled away from the Zeros.

It was a tense flight home with some planes damaged and all of us low on fuel. I was the last of our group to land and my tank was empty as I rolled to a stop. A crowd of pilots, mechanics, marines and soldiers swarmed over the plane, hauling me out of the cockpit and thumping me on the back. Barber, too, had had a field day. In addition to the other bomber, he had shot down two Zeros. We lost only one man.

That night we dined on steak, bamboo shoots and cold beer. And from the commander of U.S. Naval forces in the South Pacific came a message: "Congratulations Major Mitchell and his hunters. Sounds as though one of the ducks in their bag was a peacock."

It wasn't until after the war that we learned the full results of our mission. The bomber shot down by Barber had crashed in the sea, and two Japanese admirals were rescued, badly injured, from the wreckage. The other bomber was found in the jungle—and with it the body of Admiral Yamamoto, still clutching his ceremonial sword.

When his ashes were returned to Tokyo, millions of Japanese turned out for his state funeral. It was the greatest display of national mourning for an admiral since the funeral of Lord Nelson after Trafalgar.

A month after Yamamoto's death, Tokyo radio finally admitted that he had been killed. But for the duration of the war the United States revealed no details.

There were two reasons for this silence. One, it was feared that the meticulously-planned interception might make the enemy realize their code had been broken. The other was, for me, poignantly personal.

Only two months after the Yamamoto mission, my brother Charlie led a flight on a strafing raid against the same Kahili airfield on Bougainville. He was shot down—at almost the same spot where I had shot down Yamamoto. But Charlie survived, and was sent to a prison camp.

The U.S. Government did not reveal that I had killed Yamamoto for fear the Japanese would take reprisals against Charlie. He died of gangrene—only two weeks before U.S. Marines liberated the prison.

As I stood with my family at Charlie's funeral, I realized more than ever before the tragedy and futility of war. How ironic, I thought, that I should shoot down Admiral Yamamoto over Kahili—and that Charlie should be shot down at virtually the same spot.

I wondered sadly if mankind, which had reasoned its way to the atom, might not one day reason its way to a true peace.

A Woman's World

• Show me a woman whose home is always ready for unexpected visitors, and I'll show you a woman who's too tired to entertain.

• What's done is done—for about five minutes.

• The trouble with gourmet cooking is that by the time your children are old enough to eat it, nothing in the recipes is on your husband's diet.

• If the shoe fits, ask for it in another colour.

• No matter what the critics say, it's hard to believe that a television programme which keeps four children quiet for an hour can be all bad.

• Where is a woman with rollers in her hair in public going that's so much more important than where she is now?

• Laugh and the world laughs with you. Cry and you get what you want.

—Beryl Pfizer, *Ladies' Home Journal*

Night Train to Chittagong

By Donald David

IT WAS Bengal, 1942, a dark time for India. At our regimental forward base depot in Dacca, the adjutant handed Captain N. and me a set of identical papers, sealed and top secret. We were on our way to join the regiment at Chittagong and we had a dangerous railway journey ahead of us. "I can't offer you any escort," the adjutant said. "I haven't a man to spare. But these dispatches must reach our commanding officer as soon as possible. We aren't in wireless contact, so I must depend on you two."

By this time Singapore had fallen, Malaya was over-run and Japanese columns, driving through Burma, were poised to attack Assam, the gateway to India. Added to this threat from the east, the country harboured another menace within itself—militant activists demanding immediate independence for India.

The vast majority of Indians were loyal to the British Government, but a small, articulate group of political extremists detested the British even more than the Japanese aggressors. Long years of patronizing rebuffs had bred hatred of British rule, and pro-Axis riots were beginning to hamstring the desperate efforts of the military.

Special Risk. Our journey involved a night on the train and a crossing of the great Brahmaputra River—in ordinary circumstances, just a tiring ride of some 200 miles. But now there was the hazard of encountering "goondas"—bands of hooligans, revolutionaries and thieves—carrying long matchets. They often waylaid trains to rob and murder white occupants.

The adjutant was nervous. "These dispatches contain the names of known Japanese sympathizers in Chittagong who, in the event of a Jap breakthrough, would be a ready-made fifth column," he said. "I've

made two identical copies so that . . ." His meaning was plain. If one of us fell foul of the goondas, the other might get through.

Captain N., a former tea planter, had little use for Indian aspirations and was scornful of the adjutant's caution. "I'd like to see any goonda interfere with me," he growled.

I shared the captain's scorn, but for different reasons. A young sub-altern, I was full of pride in British arms. If the "thin red line" had controlled the Indian masses for centuries, there was no reason now for an armed British officer to fear a few underfed zealots with knives.

At the station, Captain N. and I threaded our way through the swarming crowd and entered our respective compartments—his near the engine and mine at the rear. (More caution on the adjutant's part!) I opened the windows of my carriage and, as the train lurched out of the station, poured myself a drink—whisky and cold water out of a Thermos. Then I lay down on my bunk and fell asleep.

What woke me I do not know. The train was motionless, and the dim light in the compartment had gone out. A mosquito seemed to be droning near my ear—louder, louder, louder. Suddenly I sat bolt upright. I had heard that noise once

DONALD DAVID, 46, served in India for five years during the war. Married, he now lives near Winchester where he teaches British constitutional history at the Apprentices' College of the Royal Army Pay Corps.

before. It was the voice of a mob—an eerie, mindless sound like the roaring of the sea, but with a shrill counterpoint of hatred.

We had stopped at a large station. The platform was a swaying mass of figures. *"Jai Hind!"* the mob was yelling ("Free India!"—the slogan of all Indian nationalists). I closed the windows and ran to the door on the other side. No one was visible.

A revolver cracked, once, twice, then twice more in rapid succession. I jumped down on to the track and looked up the long, curved line of the train. Suddenly the door to Captain N.'s compartment burst open, and a mass of struggling figures spilt out. The figures dispersed and, in the grey light of early dawn, I could make out a body on the ground. I was alone.

At that instant I felt my arm gripped. I whipped round, prepared to sell my life dearly, and confronted a terrified middle-aged Eurasian, a half-caste of mixed English and Indian blood. His equally terrified wife cringed at his side. "For God's sake, Mr. Officer, help us!" the man gasped.

"What's going on?"

"The goondas are attacking the Europeans on the train. They are working their way down from the engine. We shall all be murdered. Help us, sahib! In God's name, what shall we do?"

At 22 years of age, without experience in mob control, I didn't know. The cockiness I had shared with Captain N. died with him. But I couldn't admit my ignorance and fear, even to myself. I was British, a decision-maker (the Eurasian's use of "sahib" implied this).

"Quick, into my carriage!" They scrambled in. I followed, locked doors and windows, and sat down. I had no idea what to do next. I lit a cigarette. Trying to look impassive, I offered the Eurasian one, but he stared at me without comprehension. I felt my resentment rising as I looked at his ashen countenance. No man likes to see his own weakness reflected in another's face.

Crash!

An axe was being used on the door—blow after blow rained against it. I knew it could not last long, but with the crisis upon me I felt calmer. I reviewed the courses open to me. I could wait for them to burst in and slaughter us, as they surely would. I could open the window and fire at them, as Captain N. had done. Or perhaps I could persuade them that the police or military were on their way. A faint hope, but better than certain death.

Decision. I approached the door. The Eurasian, realizing my intention, sprang at me and clawed my arm, gibbering in the urgency of his terror and despair. I shook him off, and he sprawled against the bunk.

I opened the window. Immediately outside, the axe wielder paused, his axe raised in mid-stroke.

Just behind him, directing operations, stood three men, dressed in the invariable uniform of white trousers, white open-necked shirt and white forage-cap. Behind them stretched a sea of yelling, expectant faces.

I addressed the nearest of the three leaders, a dark, intense youth; a student, perhaps, from some university.

"You can't come in here," I said. "This is a first-class compartment."

The young man stared. "How dare you, a foreigner, tell us what we cannot do in our own country?"

Last Chance. We gazed at each other, a young Indian and an Englishman of about the same age. Had I been older, more set in my beliefs, I might have reacted differently. As it was, I had an uneasy feeling his question made sense.

"What is it you want?"

"We want to travel to the river— in *this* compartment."

This was my last chance. A wrong decision could mean a horrible death for the two Eurasians who had trusted me, death as well for many who would face treachery if the papers I carried failed to reach their destination. I looked at the speaker for a long moment, and something I seemed to see in his eyes gave me hope. I stepped back and opened the door.

With deliberate dignity the three mounted the steps and entered the carriage. The last one turned and spoke swiftly to the waiting crowd, four of whom detached themselves and followed him. Dark, unsmiling men, gaunt with hunger and bitterness, they crowded into the compartment, waiting for orders. They kept their hands behind their backs, but I knew what they held.

As the train pulled out of the station, I realized that all that stood between us and death was my own persuasiveness. No other help was possible now.

The dark youth opened the interrogation: "Where are you going?"

I explained.

"Why should you expect us Indians to fight your battles for you?"

The Japanese, I tried to tell him, were no respecters of persons. If they conquered India, they would enslave the whole population, native and European, whatever their political opinions.

"Even if that were true, why should we care? We are slaves now, to you British. Millions of us are starving and in rags. What could the Japanese do to us worse than you and your countrymen have already done?"

I had never looked at it that way, but I could see his point. Still, I didn't yield. I told him what the Japanese had done in their conquered territories.

"I do not believe you. The Japanese are Orientals like ourselves. They will welcome us as allies—we are fighting the same enemy."

How many hours we argued, I do not know. But I knew I had to keep talking whether I was making any impression or not. And, as we talked, I began to realize that the young man was uncertain of his theories—he seemed to need to talk to convince himself.

His companions required no such stimulus. Older, more sullen, they wanted to get the business over. Their instinct was to kill, to wipe out the hated enemy. But the young man was their leader. He had been to university. He was India's future. They would not act without him.

Looking back now, 25 years later, I can see the young Indian and myself in clearer perspective. We were playing cards with death as the stake; but the bloom of youth and idealism had not quite left us, and we still believed in reason. I wanted desperately to change the young man's poor opinion of my people; he burned to show me the error of my countrymen's ways. Then, as always, the hope of the world lay in the meeting of young people of different races—before their attitudes harden, before they identify themselves completely with their nation and background. Our conversation was just such a meeting.

We talked on.

Then, suddenly, the balance of power was reversed—the train came to an abrupt halt and from outside came the sound of running feet and British voices shouting commands. The door was flung open. An enormous sergeant shouldered in, followed by an Indian non-commissioned officer. Behind these two I could see a platoon of troops ranged along the side of the train.

The sergeant stared at me incredulously. "You all right, sir? We heard about the ambush. Never expected to find anyone alive. I'll take these scoundrels to the civil police. You'll be making a charge, of course?"

I looked round the compartment. The Eurasian was transformed. Fear had left him, hatred now suffused his face. Without a word to me, he dragged his wife from the compartment. Pausing before the raiders he spat out one word: "Bastards!"

I looked at the others. The hatchet men stood dully. They would accept whatever fate had in store for them. The two older goondas likewise seemed fatalistic; whether I charged them or not would not alter their attitudes. The battle I had to win was for the mind of the young man.

Again, I read my answer in his eyes—eyes that appealed to me not for mercy but for understanding. I knew then that my next few words would be decisive. This was the end of his youth—the time for final alignment. Would he become a rabid hater of "foreigners" like his companions, or an influence for moderation and sanity?

I turned to the sergeant. "No," I said, "there will be no charge."

Two young men had come of age that day.

HUMOUR
IN UNIFORM

In Celle, Germany, the British military hospital is quite a distance from the married quarters and a special bus is run by the authorities to take expectant mothers for their weekly check-ups. The young mothers-to-be have named their military conveyance "The Blunder Bus."   —R. H.

A civic dignitary, about to be taken on his first flight in an air force jet plane, was being briefed on how to use the emergency ejector seat. "Who bales out first, the passenger or the pilot?" he asked.

"The passenger," replied the briefing officer. "But if the pilot tells you to eject and you say, 'Eh?'—you'll be talking to yourself!"   —AP

After a strenuous ten-day exercise, a group of off-duty Naval officers were gathered in the shade on a tiny island in the Mediterranean. A small refreshment stand had been set up, and by the time the chaplain from one of the aircraft carriers had arrived, all the seats were taken except those round one table sitting in lone splendour at the top of a small rise.

The chaplain sat down there.

Up bustled a flag-lieutenant. "Sorry, sir, these seats are reserved for the staff."

Wearily the chaplain asked, "Whose staff?"

"Why, sir, the admiral and ..."

"Son," interrupted the padre, "I'm on God's staff, and until someone comes along senior to Him, I'm not moving."   —C. H. M.

An inquisitive woman was questioning my brother, home on leave, about his military experiences. She asked him about his rank, medals if any, length of service and so forth, winding up with, "You are with the Army, aren't you?"

"No, madam," he replied gravely. "I've been agin 'em all the way."
                    —Mary Peters

My naval radio crew, housed in a tent on a bluff, was trying to carry on despite heavy bombing by enemy planes.

When I heard one bomb whistling through the air terrifyingly close, I bellowed, "Hit the deck!"

The bomb exploded a mere 30 feet away, showering the tent with shrapnel, stones and earth. We got to our feet coughing and shaking. Remembering my training, by the dim light of a torch I called the roll. As I ran down the list I received a steady chorus of "Here, sir." Then I called out the last name, "Taylor." There was no answer.

Fearing the worst, with my voice pitched in a higher key, I called out again, "Taylor!"

From the shadows came an answer, "That's *you*, sir."   —Kenneth Taylor

Christmas Eve at Frontstalag 122

*Starvation and threats
could not suppress the faith
and loyalty of these resourceful prisoners*

By Gilbert Renault

THE *Sonderführer's* cold gaze ran over the 500 or so women prisoners gathered in the yard. In his tightly buttoned green uniform, he was the embodiment of the Nazi type: tall, fair, with a long, thin face, chiselled features and expressionless grey-blue eyes. His neat dress and rigid bearing were in sharp contrast to the emaciated,

dirty, ragged group assembled for roll call.

This was the morning of December 9, 1943, and it was the second time that my mother and sisters had seen the prison camp commander. The first time had been shortly after their arrival at *Frontstalag 122*—the screening camp at Royallieu—six weeks before. On that occasion, the *Sonderführer* had announced that one of the men had tried to escape from the camp during the night. "The prisoner was caught by the dogs," he snarled, "and shot down

COLONEL GILBERT RENAULT, "Rémy," was leader of the French underground network, *Confrérie Notre-Dame*, during the Second World War. He is the author of many books about the Resistance.

with a machine-gun. The same thing will happen to anyone who tries to follow his example!"

This time, the *Sonderführer* looked just as menacing, and the women lined up before him knew why. The previous day, a group of them had attacked one of the female guards. "If the culprits are not denounced immediately," he said in even, metallic tones, "there will be no more letters or parcels—and there might be more severe sanctions later on."

None of the prisoners spoke.

"As a measure of reprisal," declared the *Sonderführer* harshly, "the whole barracks will be deprived of food for the next 24 hours."

Turning on his heel, he marched off towards his office. Slowly, the prisoners filed back to their rooms.

Arrest. My mother and five sisters had belonged to the intelligence network, *Confrérie Notre-Dame,* which I had created in Occupied France, on de Gaulle's orders, in November 1940. The Gestapo watched them for some time, hoping to pick me up when I came to see them. But the Germans finally lost patience, arrested them and sent them to *Frontstalag 122*.

On arrival they were assigned to Room 9, whose 84 square yards housed 48 prisoners. The only light came from a single frosted-glass window which was permanently shut. On either side of a central aisle were two rows of double-decker bunks built of mis-shapen planks; on each bunk was a straw mattress caked with filth. The women slept on their sides, two to a mattress, covered only by two thin blankets and separated from their neighbours by a space about 15 inches wide.

Among the inmates were simple country women, aristocrats, workers, schoolteachers and prostitutes. Besides members of the Resistance, there were women who had been arrested for other offences or simply picked up in a police round-up.

"What worried us most that morning," my sister Maisie told me long afterwards, "was the thought that there would be no more parcels. Each of us received two a month, one of clothing and another of food, which kept us from starvation. But this time we had something else on our minds."

At the end of November, Mother, my sisters and six other prisoners— among them Marie Talet, ex-headmistress of a girls' school, who was later liquidated by the Nazis—had decided that Room 9 was going to have a Christmas crèche. They had sewing kits that would enable them to make the figures, using any scrap of fabric they could lay their hands on. But they needed other materials that only came in the parcels.

They also needed the parcels for warmth. It was so cold in the room that the prisoners had to keep the stove burning all day long. Marie Talet, who had been appointed room-chief by the Germans, had entrusted Maisie with the task of keeping the fire going. For this, the parcel wrappings were essential; the room was allotted only 20 pieces of wood a day, and these burned up in no time at all. Once, when she saw that the fire was dying out, Marie gave up one of the planks under her mattress. "It's softer like this," she said—so soft, in fact, that half her mattress sagged in mid-air.

True to his promise, the *Sonderführer* cut off the prisoners' rations—thin soup and a lump of grey bread—for 24 hours. But for some reason he did not carry out his threat of stopping the parcels, and soon the "conspirators," as they called themselves, were hard at work on the crèche.

Secrets. Mother, with four friends and her daughters, sewed together odd bits of fabric and twisted multi-coloured strands of wool. It had been agreed that there would be 48 figures, one for each of the room's occupants. First there would be the Holy Family, then the ass and the ox, the Kings, a good number of shepherds, and one figure for each of France's provinces. There must also be an angel, white and gold, to put on top of the crèche. The crèche itself would be about 20 inches high and three feet wide, and each figure would have a label sewn to its costume: "Royallieu, Christmas 1943."

Only the plotters themselves knew the secret. My sister Jacqueline's job was to search the parcel wrappings for anything that could be used for the crèche. Irène Tillion, considered the intellectual of the group, was given the task of composing the *Hymn of Frontstalag 122, Room 9.*

All was ready by Christmas Eve. The night was icy cold. The prisoners were in deep despair, but the conspirators of Room 9 were determined to bring back hope to the hearts of their companions. At nine o'clock, Marie Talet slipped to the door at one end of the room. To attract the attention of the other inmates, she clapped her hands as she had so often done at school. "Children!" she called.

Her voice was too soft to be heard by most of the prisoners who were already lying, two by two, on their mattresses. Marie clapped once more and repeated in a louder voice: "Children!" This time several heads were raised. "My children, tonight is Christmas Eve."

Now all the occupants of Room 9 were listening. Meanwhile, the conspirators at the other end of the room were putting up a piece of corrugated cardboard lined with magnificent red paper. Real straw taken from a cheese box had been made into a thatched roof. With an eyedropper my sister Jacqueline was filling halved walnut shells with oil from sardine tins. In each shell she placed a tiny wick made of wisps of cotton-wool.

"We are all separated from those we love and with whom we have so often shared the joy of Christmas

Eve," Marie Talet was saying. "To-night our real Family is here in this room, and our ties are those of our common misery."

As she spoke, the conspirators were putting into place the 48 little figures—the infant Jesus, dressed in a postage-stamp size shift of white linen, the Virgin with a veil over her head. Opposite Mary knelt Joseph, his face almost hidden by a brown beard made from strands of wool. In front of the crib were placed the three Kings wearing crowns of silver paper. Next came the shepherds, gazing in wonder at the Child, while the angel was hung above the crèche in a long white robe, with the flag of France in his arms.

When everything was in place, Marie raised her right hand and the conspirators began to sing. Startled, the inmates turned towards the other end of the room. There, before their astonished eyes, stood the crèche, glowing in the semi-darkness with the soft light of the walnut-shell candles; and the conspirators sang on.

At the end, Marie Talet cried in a vibrant voice: "Long live France!"

Gripped by an emotion which many of them had never known before, all the women—even those from sordid hotels or the Paris slums—echoed her cry: "Long live France!" Here, in *Frontstalag 122,*

where the "shepherds" stood on watchtowers in their steel helmets and with machine-guns, these lost women found once more the hopeful years of their youth. Slipping from their bunks they fell to their knees and sobbed.

Suddenly, they heard the sound of heavy boots approaching. Raising her hand once more, Marie Talet got everyone singing.

Alleluia!—The child is born!
Sound the clarions and the
*   trumpets;*
Alleluia, the Child is born!
He brings Liberty!

The door burst open and the *Sonderführer* stood before them. Trim as usual in his uniform, the master of *Frontstalag 122* looked into the faces of the thin, dirty women who watched him silently, prepared for the worst. His cold gaze fell on the crèche, surrounded by its luminous, flickering garland of makeshift candles. On the roof of the crèche the golden-haired angel held the tricolour flag which silently spoke its defiance of the conqueror.

The *Sonderführer* bit his thin lips and stiffened. As the women watched unbelievingly, he clicked his heels, raised his hand to his cap, and stood frozen in salute. Then, turning on his heel, he left, closing the door softly behind him.

It is truly not the value but the worth of a thing that is important, as in the case of an inexpensive but strategically placed button.—Patricia Clafford

A Reader's Digest
'First Person' Award

The Day the Atomic Age Was Born

By Herbert Anderson
as told to J. D. Ratcliff

OF THE EVENTS that have changed man's destiny—the invention of the stone axe, the discovery of fire, the drift into the Industrial Revolution—few can be pinpointed in time. But one, possibly the greatest of all, can be timed to the minute. At 3.36 p.m. on December 2, 1942, the world entered the Atomic Age. And I was one of 40-odd witnesses.

The setting was hardly auspicious: a bleak, draughty, dimly lit squash court under the abandoned and crumbling stadium at the University of Chicago's athletic field. There, within a pile of uranium and graphite bricks the size of a small house, neutrons were being born at the rate of thousands of millions each second and hurled out at velocities of 18,000 miles a second. Every one that hit the heart of another uranium atom shattered that atom to produce *two* neutrons. Thus, every few minutes, the silent, violent storm was doubling itself in history's first nuclear chain reaction.

We were too awed to speak. The silence was broken only by the staccato rattle of counters keeping track of neutron production. All our advance reasoning indicated that we were safe. Yet we were pushing into territory never before explored. There was at least a chance that the pile would get out of control; that we would be destroyed and a large, thickly settled portion of Chicago would be converted into a radioactive wasteland.

Science sometimes moves at a plodding pace. But with atomic fission, events had moved at breakneck speed. Only four years before, at Kaiser Wilhelm Institute for Chemistry in Berlin, nuclear chemist Otto Hahn and his young assistant, Fritz Strassmann, had bombarded uranium with neutrons from an external source. Afterwards, chemical analysis showed that barium and other substances not there before had appeared as from nowhere and were mixed with the uranium! But if the two experimenters thought that they had split the heavy uranium into barium and other lighter elements, they weren't prepared to say so.

Interpretation fell to a former

December 2, 1942: the scientists on the squash-court balcony are about to witness the world's first nuclear chain reaction. At the control panel was Herbert Anderson, then 28, who had just earned his doctorate in physics. He is now a professor at the University of Chicago

Hahn colleague, Lise Meitner. In Sweden, during the Christmas holidays of 1938, she and her nephew, Otto Frisch, discussed Hahn's data. Possibly, their two brilliant minds concluded, these findings weren't so mysterious after all. Their friend Niels Bohr, the great Danish physicist, had visualized the nucleus of an atom as a liquid drop. If bombardment added an extra neutron to the nucleus, it might become unstable, elongate and divide. The electric repulsion between the two new droplets would be enormous. Within days, Frisch was testing.

When each heavy uranium atom split into lighter atoms, there was a fantastic release of 200 million electron volts. If multiplied by millions of millions it meant a power yield undreamed of. The world might no longer have to depend on the fossil fuels alone—coal, oil, natural gas—and face an energy famine when they were gone.

Still, big questions remained. Could you smash an atom with one neutron and get a yield of *two* neutrons that would go on to smash again and produce four, eight, and so on? Moving slowly, such a chain reaction would produce heat which could be converted into power. If the reaction proceeded fast enough, you would have a monster of a bomb.

A fear was with all of us. The

German pioneers had certainly foreseen the possibilities of such a bomb. If the Nazis got it first, other countries would be at their mercy. This was therefore a race we had to win. We had to find out if a chain reaction was possible.

Most of the work on "The Metallurgical Project" (our code name) would be concentrated at the University of Chicago. Arthur Holly Compton, of that institution, would head it, and refugee Italian scientist Enrico Fermi would be charged with building CP-1—Chicago Pile No. 1. As we started work, we had only question marks. We knew that natural uranium spontaneously emits a few neutrons. But they travel too fast to cause fission—like a fast-moving golf ball that skims over a cup, whereas a slow-moving one would drop in.

Graphite seemed the best available means of slowing these neutrons. Perhaps some sort of lattice could be arranged—bits of uranium surrounded by graphite? Neutrons from one bit of uranium would pass through the graphite, slow down, strike into atoms in another bit of uranium and cause fission.

There were catches in the process. Any impurities in the graphite would act as neutron sponges and put out any atomic fire. And there was no graphite as pure as we needed, anywhere—and we'd want it in 100-ton lots. The problem with uranium was much the same.

Industry and universities threw themselves with admirable energy into making the absolutely pure stuff, although we couldn't tell them *why* it was so urgent. By the spring of 1942, droplets of uranium metal, uranium oxide and graphite began to arrive. Pile building began (we were to build 30 experimental piles to provide basic data before beginning work on the big one).

Space-Age Sphere. On November 7, Fermi indicated that we were ready. Enough graphite, uranium metal and uranium oxide had been accumulated for the big pile. Work was shared out. Walter Zinn was in charge of the day shift. They would plane and shape the 40,000 graphite blocks—some of these were drilled to contain slugs of uranium metal or uranium oxide. I headed the night shift. We would lay the slippery bricks in exact patterns just as fast as they could be produced.

Preliminary calculations indicated that the most effective shape for our pile would be a sphere 24 feet in diameter. The most active uranium we had—the metal—would be in the centre, with the less active oxide further out. The great sphere began to grow: a layer of graphite, then a layer of graphite bricks containing uranium, and so on.

For safety controls, we relied principally on three wooden rods, each with strips of cadmium metal tacked on, running through the pile. Cadmium, the best of neutron sponges, would dampen any atomic conflagration. One rod would be controlled electrically. A second, the "zip" rod, had to be pulled out of the pile by rope; release the rope and it would slip in. The third was for fine control, and would be hand-operated to achieve the level of neutron activity wanted. Any one of the three rods would quench the atomic fire—unless something unforeseen happened.

Facing Death. Three men would be stationed on top of the scaffolding surrounding the pile—a "suicide squad." They would have great flasks of cadmium solution to quench a runaway reaction. "If things get away from us," Fermi told them, "break the flasks. But watch me, and don't do it until I drop dead. If you do it before, I'll use a sledge-hammer on you!"

By the time my shift took over on December 1, we were at the forty-eighth layer, and Fermi had calculated that layer 51 would complete the job. He read what was on my mind. There would be the greatest temptation to pull out the control rods and be the first in the world to observe a chain reaction. "When you have finished layer 51," he directed, "lock those rods in place. Everyone be here at eight tomorrow morning."

Morning dawned chill and grey, with a dust of snow on the ground. General Eisenhower had launched his North African campaign. The battle for Guadalcanal was in its final victorious phases. Work was under way on super-secret atomic-bomb

plants, on the faith that a chain reaction was possible. If our reactor worked, it had the potential not only for death, but for ending a nightmarish war and saving millions of lives.

By eight o'clock, we had all filed into our places. I was at a control panel to record instrument readings. Zinn was to pull out the zip rod. George Weil manned the all-important hand rod. The suicide squad was at the ready. Observers stood on a small balcony where spectators had formerly watched squash games. The great show was about to begin.

Agonizing Hours. At 9.45, Fermi ordered the electrically controlled rod to be pulled out. There was a slight whirring of motors, and the clicking of counters could be heard. Neutron activity was rising. Fermi's mild grey eyes were on the pen as it moved upwards on a piece of graph paper before levelling off. Hardly aware of the presence of others, he manipulated a slide rule. Everything was going according to plan.

At ten, he ordered Zinn to pull out the zip rod. There was another increase in neutron production—but again nothing massive.

At 10.37, Fermi directed Weil: "Pull the hand rod out to 13 feet." The counter began to roar. Anxious faces looked at the pen sweeping upwards. Fermi indicated that it would level off at a certain point, and it did. From time to time he ordered Weil to pull the rod out another few inches. Each time there was an upsurge of neutron activity, and our tension rose proportionately —to an almost unbearable pitch.

Then the spell was broken. "Let's go to lunch," said Fermi. It was like Wellington suggesting a lunch break at the Battle of Waterloo. All rods went back in, and counters fell silent, except for an occasional feeble click. Even at rest the pile produced 100,000 neutrons a second.

New Era. At two o'clock, we began again, more rapidly. At three, the counters had to be recalibrated —slowed down to dampen the rattle and give meaning to their sounds. Further, the pen was going off the graph paper. At 3.19, Fermi ordered the hand rod to be withdrawn another foot. He glanced at the graph, consulted his slide rule, then turned to Compton, standing beside him. "The next foot should do it," he said. At 3.36, the hand rod was withdrawn a final foot. And, minutes later, he spoke again: "This time it won't level off. The curve is exponential"—the activity would go on doubling and redoubling.

For 17 agonizing minutes the atomic storm raged, growing increasingly violent. The pile was heating up. The first chain reaction was under way. In ominous silence mankind was entering a new age. Fission, we knew, would create new radioactive elements—and with the greatest rapidity. Our pile could be safe one moment and deadly the next. Understandably, worry was written on many faces. Eyes were on radiation meters, which showed that we were rapidly approaching danger levels.

At 3.53 Fermi turned to Zinn. "Zip in," he said. As the rod slipped into the pile, activity diminished rapidly. The great drama was coming to an end. We had made a safe journey into the unknown.

IF THE world is depressed by the fact that two atomic bombs were dropped 32 months later, it might take heart from the enormous benefits that have accrued from fission. Much of medical science has been revolutionized, and the pace of other research quickened. Britain is already deriving nearly 14 per cent of her electric power from the atom, and today the U.S. Atomic Energy Commission is spending more on peaceful atomic pursuits than on weaponry.

On that bitter, blustery winter afternoon over a quarter of a century ago, history was changed. Possibly it was for the worse. Hopefully, time will prove it was for the better.

EVERY morning for the past 11 years, a salesman has got up at six o'clock to take his dog for a walk. Recently, the dog died. The next morning, the man stared at the ceiling for a few moments, then nudged his wife. "Hey," he said. "Fancy a walk?"   —H. C.

The physicists who took part in the building of the first atomic pile in 1942 at a 4th anniversary reunion. Back row, left to right: N. Hilberry, Samuel Allison, Thomas Brill, Robert Nobles, Warren Nyer, and Marvin Wilkenberg. Middle row, left to right: Harold Agnew, William Sturm, Harold Lichtenberger, Leona W. Marshall, and Leo Szilard. Front row, left to right: Enrico Fermi, Walter Zinn, Albert Wattenberg, and Herbert Anderson.

Resistance Heroine of Two World Wars

By Virginie Henry

Twice her beloved France suffered German occupation. And twice Emilienne Moreau-Evrard refused to accept defeat

It was October 1941. At the rear of a small, brick house at 24 avenue du Quatre-Septembre in Lens, a mining town in north-east France, a small, slender woman in her forties was busy in her kitchen. But it wasn't the evening meal Emilienne Moreau-Evrard was preparing, standing at her stove. She was wrapping bundles of clandestine newspapers for distribution.

Suddenly the doorbell rang. Feverishly, Emilienne thrust her bundles under the sink, then peeped through a front window. She counted at least ten green uniforms. When she opened the door, a Wehrmacht general, wearing the Iron Cross, clicked his heels, bowed and walked into the living-room, followed by his escort, which lined up at attention behind him. The colour

drained from Emilienne's cheeks, but the general was smiling.

"Madame Moreau," he said in a friendly voice, "don't you recognize me?"

"No, not at all," stammered Emilienne.

"But I haven't forgotten *you*. When I knew you, I was only a lieutenant, back in 1915, in Loos-en-Gohelle where I was garrisoned. You were very brave, and they say you won many decorations. I have come to see them."

Madame Moreau-Evrard heaved a sigh of relief and hurried off to look for a small leather-bound chest. Then she watched astonished as a top-ranking officer of the victorious German Army respectfully handled the most extraordinary collection of medals ever earned by a woman: the French Croix de

Guerre 1915, the Legion of Honour (military class), the Combattant's Cross and, from the British, the Royal Red Cross, the Officer of the Order of Saint John of Jerusalem and, rare for a Frenchwoman, the Military Medal.

Their recipient stood silently as the escort saluted her. Then, after promising Emilienne she would have nothing to fear as long as he was in Lens, the general turned on his heel and marched out.

He probably assumed that France's most decorated woman would sit out the new war resting on her laurels. And he would have been greatly surprised in 1945 to inspect the new honours reaped by his protégé in her second offensive against the Germans: the Croix de Guerre 1939–45, the Cross of Officer in the Legion of Honour and, above all, the green and black ribbon denoting a Companion of the Liberation—the supreme honour of the French Resistance, won by only six women.

Emilienne's warrior career began suddenly in October 1914. She was only 16 then, a beautiful, dark-eyed brunette, when her home in Loos-en-Gohelle near Lens became the centre of bloody combat. The Moreau house, standing on the village square midway between the French and German lines, was a high building topped by an attic in which the girl had set up an observation post to watch the fighting. When she climbed to her look-out on October 6, 1914, she suddenly spied something metallic glinting in the sunlight on a hill on the German side.

Under cover of night, the Kaiser's troops had apparently camouflaged machine-gun nests behind the pylons at the entrance to a mine, allowing them to dominate the space between the enemy positions. Then glancing in the other direction, Emilienne saw a small detachment of French infantrymen rise out of their trenches and begin to move into the enemy trap.

Guardian Angel. In a letter of gratitude later sent to the woman who saved his life, one of those soldiers, Private Pochet, tells what happened next: "As we moved out, a young girl sprang from God knows where, ran across the village square under increasingly heavy enemy fire and shouted to us, 'Don't advance! Go back! The Germans have set a trap for you.'"

Her heroism that morning prevented a massacre, but the Allied troops withdrew a few days later leaving the Germans masters of Loos-en-Gohelle. Now Emilienne proceeded to set an example of daily resistance to the invaders. For instance, on July 14, 1915, the German commandant, fearful of demonstrations on Bastille day, posted throughout the town a "warning to the population" that display of the tricolour was forbidden, under pain of death.

At dawn that same morning,

JACK McCARTHY

Madame Emilienne Moreau-Evrard

Emilienne, her brother and sister went off on an innocent excursion into the countryside. For hours they tramped across fields, gathering flowers. The boy picked blue cornflowers, his younger sister gathered poppies, and Emilienne plucked white daisies. A few hours later, in the local cemetery, tricoloured bouquets were decorating the mass grave of the 300 villagers killed during the fighting.

That autumn the front was drawing nearer. One October evening, the earth began to shake and steel showered down on the houses and fortifications of Loos-en-Gohelle as Field-Marshal Sir Douglas Haig's Highlanders attacked the town. In Haslach, Germany, 86-year-old Wilhem Dietz, one of the German defenders of Loos, is still living. He describes the battle in these words:

"A few of us were trying to stem the Allied advance towards the centre of the town. Suddenly, I saw a girl under the machine-gun fire, running in front of the invaders, pointing out the weak points in our defence, carrying munitions and food, giving water to the soldiers, bandaging and comforting the wounded. She was everywhere, like a goddess of Vengeance." That girl was Emilienne Moreau.

She offered the only room still intact in her house to the Scottish regiment as an emergency hospital. Day and night for a week, Emilienne helped treat the 400 Scottish wounded. The regimental medic reported Emilienne's heroic conduct and, overnight, she became a celebrity. On October 7, 1915, Marshal Haig wrote to her to express his "sincere admiration." Marshal Foch cited her in his general orders, and all Paris paid tribute to her.

With the war's end, the heroine retired into obscurity. She married a childhood sweetheart, Just Evrard. Their life with their two sons was happy and uneventful. But when Nazi forces invaded northern France in the spring of 1940, Emilienne and all her family enlisted in this new struggle.

In those days, Monsieur and

Madame Moreau-Evrard sold disinfectants and fire-fighting equipment to local authorities in the region—a perfect cover for clandestine operations. When the Gestapo enquired into the frequent journeys of Emilienne and Just, someone in the villages they had been to was always able to produce an order form for a fire extinguisher as justification for the visit.

Enemy Alerted. But in September 1941, the synthetic-petrol factory in Liéven blew up only a few days after Just Evrard's passage through the town. He was arrested on suspicion and held for seven months before being released. Three days later the Moreau-Evrards came home to find a printed form under the door: "Sir, kindly report to the Commandant with your identity papers and a change of linen."

Emilienne knew what this meant. She packed Just's suitcase. Urging him to escape, she pushed him out of the house.

Shortly after her husband got away, a price was put on Emilienne's head by the Gestapo. So, with the help of a Polish interpreter working for the German Army, she managed to, obtain an *ausweis* (pass) to the unoccupied zone, and rejoined her husband in Lyons.

"Brutus," one of the Resistance's most important espionage networks, had set up its headquarters in Lyons. Emilienne was to carry out for it more than a hundred underground liaison missions.

While many agents ended their careers within months in Nazi concentration camps, she contrived to outwit the vigilance of the Gestapo for nearly two years.

Luck played a part in her success. Early in 1944, for example, she was sent to Thonon-les-Bains to transmit highly important orders to "Victor," the director of the city's hotel school. When the train pulled into the station, she noticed that the platform swarmed with grey-green uniforms. At the exit check-point, Emilienne plunged her hand into her handbag and pulled out at random one of two false identity cards. It carried the name of Catherine Robin.

The men at the exit let her through. She was heading towards the hotel school when a bicycle slowed down beside her. "The Préfecture café," the cyclist murmured. "Go in the back way."

In the café, a few minutes later, she heard the news: "they" had arrested Victor that morning. Among the names they found in his address book was that of a certain Jeanne Poirier, the name on Emilienne's other identity card. They had been looking for *her* at the station.

But luck alone is not enough to explain Madame Moreau-Evrard's success as a Resistance agent. The job also called for indomitable physical toughness—a quality little expected in a housewife well past 40. On one operation in 1943, she spent three days in a hide-out with nothing to eat but raw carrots.

Emilienne's bravery was such that she was entrusted with increasingly important missions. When the Resistance learned that the Nazis were building V1 rocket launching pads in the Pas-de-Calais, she was sent to find out the exact locations. The job would have been dangerous for anyone, but for Madame Moreau-Evrard, wanted by the Gestapo, it was madness.

She had, it is true, the advantage of knowing a host of people in the region who could filter information to her. Her brother-in-law, Georges Loir, owner of a small haulage firm in Lillers requisitioned by the Germans, told her that his lorries were often used to carry building materials to the village of Thérouanne, where the Nazis had been setting up secret installations. A doctor who specialized in rehabilitating handicapped persons was one of the rare Frenchmen authorized to circulate freely in the region. To Emilienne, he described the "mysterious" buildings he had seen in another village, Rely.

The names of both villages were immediately transmitted to the Brutus network. A few weeks later, RAF bombers smashed the Thérouanne and Rely installations.

Danger was growing for the Brutus network's liaison agent. By December 1943, she was wanted simultaneously by the Germans, Petain's police and Darnand's collaborationist militia. But she succeeded in eluding them all.

Lasting Fame. After the war, Emilienne and Just returned to their quiet way of life. And yet, until her death last January, occasions arose to remind Emilienne of her glorious past. When General de Gaulle, then President of France, visited Lens in 1959, Madame Moreau-Evrard was among those chosen to greet him. The General quickly shook the hands thrust at him. Then, suddenly, he stopped: "Emilienne," he said, "let me kiss you."

Among Madame Moreau-Evrard's most fervent admirers is her grand-daughter Catherine, aged 12. One day in school, the girl was asked to write an essay on "the person you most admire." Naturally, Catherine chose her grandmother. A week later, the girl's parents were called to the school and shown the essay. "It's very good," the teacher said, "but your daughter has an over-active imagination. You should have her examined by a psychologist."

The teacher, of course, was flabbergasted to learn that every word of the girl's account was true. But then, Emilienne Moreau-Evrard's life would surprise anybody.

OVERHEARD: "Sometimes I think my mind is getting broader, but then I realize it's just my conscience stretching."
—Troy Gordon

VOLUME 101

The
Reader's Digest

NOVEMBER 1972

© 1972 The Reader's Digest Association Ltd.

The Goodhearts
of Nijmegen

By Antony Brown

*Expressing their gratitude in deeds, these kindly Dutch
people have made remembrance a way of life*

SOME place-names in southern Holland are unforgettable, dragging on your memory like barbed wire. A long time ago—or was it?—they featured in the news so prominently. Oosterbeek, headquarters in September 1944 of German military power in the west. Arnhem, where the First British Airborne Division tried to crush that power by capturing the Rhine bridges. Nijmegen, where the Guards Armoured Division and the 82nd U.S. Airborne Division took the bridge over the Waal river as the Arnhem attack foundered.

Another reason why you cannot forget the Second World War in this part of Holland is the cemeteries. Drive round the lanes outside Nijmegen (pronounced Nay may' khen) and signposts will lead you to quiet fields where, in all, about 7,000 British and Commonwealth soldiers are buried. Many of them, it occurs to me, were no older than my own children are today—my own children, who would agree with most of their generation that remembrance of the dead is less important than help for the living. Less important, it seems to me, but not *un*important.

The thought returns as I knock on the door of a house in Hatert, a prosperous suburb of Nijmegen where the legendary Peter Vermeeren has lived for the past 37 years. I am curious to meet the man who is so well known to thousands of British visitors to the war graves.

A shortish, agile man in his early seventies, he says he will drive me to the Jonkerbos cemetery, which lies just outside the town. He has to go there anyway: he wants to lay some flowers on an airman's grave.

"Did you know him?" I ask.

No, he says, he is acting on behalf of a Dutch family who live more than 30 miles away in the province of Limburg. Each year since 1944 when the Limburg family saw the RAF pilot shot down over their farm-house, they have sent money for flowers to be put on his grave.

It seems to me 28 years is a long time to remember someone you never met. The Dutchman says that this is nothing unusual around Nijmegen.

We arrive at the cemetery and stroll for a while in the afternoon sun, watching the gardeners trimming the green lawns, pruning roses on headstones whose names and regiments read like a muffled drum-beat. Once this was a battle-field scarred with wrecked tanks.

Now it is more like a garden than a graveyard. There is a resonance in the air, almost like music.

As we stroll beneath the yew-trees, Peter Vermeeren tells me his story. During the war he was a schoolmaster near Nijmegen.

"If you haven't lived through an occupation you cannot imagine what it was like," Peter says, his eyes darkening.

For a moment you can sense what five years of Nazi occupation were like for a proud and courageous Dutch people: five years in which you could be punished for listening to the BBC, five years when mothers hardly dared watch for their older children coming home in case they had been taken off for German forced-labour gangs. After the Allied landings in 1944, the liberation of Nijmegen had been a false dawn. For months the city remained in the front line, battered mercilessly by German guns.

Peter and his family had numerous British soldiers billeted with them. "So many of the brave boys we had known were killed," he tells me. "After the war local children used to put flowers on their graves and we wrote to their parents. We made many other contacts through the British Legion. That was really the beginning of the Goodhearts family."

"The Goodhearts family?"

"A sort of society we formed in Nijmegen."

For the first time I notice a small

M. TAYLOR

An unknown soldier lies at rest in the Jonkerbos cemetery

badge in his lapel, a white cross on a red ground in a heartshape. Peter fingers the badge, explaining, "We felt it was the right symbol; a cross in a heart. It means the boys who are buried here have found a place in our hearts."

"What does the Goodhearts family do?"

Pacing around the great crescent of graves, Peter begins to tell me. How since 1945 any Commonwealth relatives coming to visit war graves have been given what amounts to the freedom of Nijmegen. How all their travel expenses once they set foot on Dutch soil have been paid by the Netherlands War Graves Committee. How some 9,500 British relatives have

been house guests of local families in Nijmegen. If someone wants to visit a grave in another part of Holland, the Nijmegen families think nothing of driving him 100 miles and more.

"They gave so much," says Peter. "What we can do seems so little."

One Nijmegen woman has a tablecloth embroidered with the signatures of some 150 relatives of the fallen who have stayed with her. For 20 years the workers in one of the biggest local factories gave a percentage of their payroll to help with fares and entertainment for poor British families—canal trips to Amsterdam, coach tours of the tulip fields in the spring.

"We try to make these visits not

just an occasion for mourning," Peter tells me. "For British and Dutch alike, they have been the beginning of treasured friendships."

Peter Vermeeren's proudest memory is of the 1956 visit paid to Nijmegen by Lieutenant-General Sir Brian Horrocks, wartime commander of XXX Corps which had spearheaded the Second Army's advance on the town. "There was a ceremonial parade and a service of remembrance—the sort of occasion on which you'd expect a general to wear all his medals and decorations. But General Horrocks didn't. He simply wore the little badge of the Goodhearts of Nijmegen."

One of the things you would perhaps expect is that war cemeteries would all look the same—yet later when Peter takes me to some of the others, I sense that the feeling of each is different. There are small, wooded cemeteries like Mook, where deer graze on a hillside and 301 British and Commonwealth servicemen lie: bigger, more formal ones like the Canadian Cemetery at Groesbeek, where 2,578 Commonwealth soldiers are buried. East of Groesbeek, the wooded hills slope to meadows, then to a church spire like a pepperpot, then up to the Reichswald forest. In the distance, a car's windscreen glints. It is hard to accept that the car is on the other side of the German frontier.

"Only now are the trees beginning to grow again after the fighting," says Peter. We stand silent, looking at the faint blur of green on the distant ridge.

"What about German war graves?" I ask.

Many of the Germans who fell here were buried in their own country, he tells me, but there is a vast German cemetery at Ijsselsteijn in Holland, where more than 30,000 German soldiers lie buried. When a British war widow visited it, she looked at it for a long time, then said to Peter, "Now there is no more hatred in our hearts."

From Groesbeek Peter takes me to Oosterbeek, on the outskirts of Arnhem, where men of the First British Airborne Division lie buried. We stroll about the quiet lawns for a while and then go to one of the brick buildings by the cemetery entrance, where the register of names of those buried here is housed.

As we browse through the books of names, a car draws up. A Dutch family—a young couple with two children—get out and walk towards the cemetery. Moving reverently between the graves, they stay for a quarter of an hour while their children play in the car park.

Before they leave, the man goes into the building and writes in the visitors' book, kept in a box next to the one with the names of those who are buried. *"Dank voor alles,"* I read. "Thank you for everything." And another, "Our liberators will never be forgotten."

I also glance over some of the

comments made by British families. "Only by seeing can one believe the beauty and peace here," writes one Norwich woman. "Our son is not buried in a foreign land," says another, "but among friends."

To help the living *and* to honour the dead. As I say good-bye to Peter, my questions about remembrance have been answered. Freedom began here not only for my generation but for my children's. Here and in all the lands where those who fought for it lie buried. As the years go by, these precious places will have a new and continuing purpose —to remind future generations that it must not happen again.

THIS ARTICLE IS BASED ON A CHAPTER IN THE AUTHOR'S BOOK "RED FOR REMEMBRANCE" (HEINEMANN)
© 1970 THE ROYAL BRITISH LEGION

Frankly Speaking

SPURRED by my wife's mastery of four languages, I applied myself to instruction book and gramophone record in a serious attempt to bone up on other languages. I made but halting progress. After two years, I found I dreaded going into the subjunctive unless I made certain beforehand that I could get out again.

Then one morning, the solution hit me right between the eyes. My mind was rejecting learning foreign languages because they would spoil the pleasure of travelling. And so the Muir Principle of Foreign Travel was formulated: a person who travels in a foreign country speaking the language well misses half the fun.

Consider food. When in Florence, after three hours pounding the galleries, you sit down in a cool trattoria and scan the alien delights—*osso buco, fettucini al burro, risotto*—what good is it to know that what is coming up is boiled bones, squashed spaghetti with a dab of butter, and rice pudding with peas in it?

And consider human contact. If, in a Madrid shop, a lady bumps into you gently and murmurs *Apartese un poco, queso de bola!* you smile your best warm, British smile at her and fervently hope that this is the start of something big. If you speak Spanish, you know that, roughly translated, she said, "Move your fat behind."

And finally, the guide books. Here, at least, a promising start has been made. The people who translate these into our language are Muir Principle men to the core. They have developed a prose style of such opacity that no information is divulged and so the reader's holiday is saved.

Here is just one example, from an English-language guide book to Rome: "Panoramas and walks for he who is romantic, he who is in love and for he who wants to soar avidly, almost to concentrate the stupendous vision of the immense city inside himself with a single hit in the eye."

—Frank Muir in *Trident* (the BEA in-flight magazine)

The Ship That Saved Malta

By George Pollock

Ohio's convoy had to breach the Axis blockade—the course of the war hung on it

WHEN the tanker SS *Ohio* was 12 hours out from the River Clyde, Captain Dudley Mason mustered his crew to read them the contents of a sealed envelope. This envelope, embossed with the Admiralty crest and marked "Not to be opened until under way," contained a letter that bore no less a signature than that of the First Lord.

The date: August 3, 1942. *Ohio* was one of 14 merchant ships in convoy WS 21S, a code number indicating that they were ostensibly bound for Suez via the Cape of Good Hope. But long before they weighed anchor, *Ohio's* crew—52 hand-picked officers and men of the Eagle Oil and Shipping Company —suspected bluff. Too much had happened for this to be a routine voyage.

First, *Ohio* was no ordinary ship. Although flying the red ensign of the Merchant Navy, she was American-owned, on loan to Britain at top-level request for just

ILLUSTRATION: CHRIS MAYGER

one voyage. Only two years old, of 14,000 tons and enormously strong welded construction, she had a maximum speed of 18 knots, half as fast again as any British tanker. Her steam pipes and machinery had been elaborately shock-proofed, and 24 army and navy gunners had come on board to man the nine anti-aircraft guns now mounted on *Ohio's* decks—a significant armament for a merchantman.

The entire crew, from 46-year-old Scots Chief Engineer Jimmy Wyld to the 17-year-old apprentices, Wilkinson and Bulmer, knew their suspicions were justified when Captain Mason read the First Lord's letter revealing *Ohio's* true destination: "Malta has for some time been in great danger. It is imperative that she should be kept supplied. She has stood up to the most violent attack from the air that has ever been made, and she needs your help in continuing the battle. Her courage is worthy of yours."

Convoy WS 21S was, in fact, to

be part of Operation Pedestal, a massive bid to break the Axis blockade of Malta. The odds were formidable—out of 17 ships in the last relief convoy, two only had reached the island. As the convoy's solitary tanker, *Ohio* and her 14,600-ton cargo—fuel oil for Malta's ships and shore installations, paraffin for her domestic needs and diesel oil for submarines based at the island—would be the enemy's prime target.

But unless some of the merchantmen, and particularly *Ohio,* got through, Malta would be forced to surrender within three weeks. Then the Mediterranean fortress, vital to cut Rommel's North African supply line, would be in Axis hands, the whole Middle East war theatre in jeopardy.

"I've no doubt whatever that you'll all do your utmost," Mason told his men. "I have absolute faith in every one of you."

Never had any convoy had such an escort: two battleships, *Nelson* and *Rodney,* four aircraft carriers—one ferrying 37 reinforcement Spitfires to Malta—seven cruisers, 32 destroyers. The lives of 23,000 seamen had been committed to this attempt to secure Malta's survival.

Cat and Mouse. On the night of August 9, the ships slipped through the Straits of Gibraltar, shrouded by fog. Bu⁺ at ten a.m. an airline pilot spotted the fleet and alerted Axis intelligence. Three hours later, what the Italians were to call the Battle of Mid-August opened

devastatingly when Kapitänleutnant Helmut Rosenbaum dived his submarine U-73 to within 500 yards of the aircraft carrier *Eagle.*

Hearing four torpedoes explode rapidly astern of *Ohio,* greaser Bill McConalogue put his head through a messroom porthole and saw *Eagle's* flight deck tilt crazily. A Hurricane fighter screamed desperately to get airborne but the heeling deck hurtled it into the sea. Others slithered after it. In eight minutes *Eagle* had vanished, taking more than a quarter of Operation Pedestal's fighter defence.

Doom-Laden Skies. "We'll be next," muttered one *Ohio* deckhand. In the ensuing 30 hours any member of Operation Pedestal might have felt the same. Torpedoes streamed up from the depths; parachute mines—the first ever experienced—showered down on them; German and Italian bombers, up to a hundred at a time, shrieked above the convoy.

One carrier was left ablaze and crippled; a destroyer was sunk, a second limped back to Gibraltar. The first of the precious merchant ships went to the bottom.

By seven p.m. on August 12, both the remaining carriers and the battleships had to turn back because they could not manoeuvre in the narrows between Sicily and Tunisia. Within an hour, an Italian submarine torpedoed two cruisers. Next in line was *Ohio.*

A torpedo slammed into her port

British troops clearing debris in Malta

side, just aft of the bridge. The explosion stopped *Ohio's* engines, wrecked the compasses and steering gear, and blasted a huge hole in the side. From deep in the tanker, blazing paraffin burst through the pumproom skylight and flamed masthead high. Captain Mason rang down to the engine room. "The pumproom's on fire, Chief. Can you get the steam smothering system going?" But Jimmy Wyld couldn't. Fire-fighting pipes were fractured.

Crewmen leapt to action. Three grabbed extinguishers and hissed foam down into the pumproom depths. Others—some with sand buckets, some with their caps—doused pools of fire which dropped from the soaring column of flame.

Alone and crippled, *Ohio* invited a *coup de grâce*. But as the bombers thundered in, the ship's gunners defied them deafeningly. From the bridge, Mason saw his apprentices, Wilkinson and Bulmer, swinging their Oerlikon guns to meet each fresh attack and thought, "Damn good boys those." Bombs whistled down, cascading water on deck. "They're putting the fire out for us!" shouted a jubilant fire-fighter.

In ten minutes it was all over; bombers driven off, fires quenched. "This was much easier than at first anticipated," commented Mason in his log. But with his ship virtually cut in half, he was still 250 miles from Malta and he knew that the bombers would be back.

Mason turned to Wyld. "Any chance of getting under way, Chief?" The engineers went below. Within 90 minutes, Wyld reported: "I'll start slowly and work her up." Gradually, so as not to break *Ohio* in two, Wyld increased speed to 16 knots. The rushing sea flooded into the great port-side hole and made *Ohio* veer unpredictably. It was now getting dark; manning the emergency steering position on the poop deck, Chief Officer Douglas Gray grimly fought to hold the tanker on course—a task he was to perform for 30 gruelling hours.

Deprived of compasses, Mason asked the destroyer *Ledbury* to guide him through the minefields back to the rest of the convoy. *Ledbury* gave him a blue pinpoint of light which Mason followed throughout the night, passing instructions to Gray at the wheel.

Around them was a panorama of slaughter. Parachute flares lit the sea between Cape Bon in Tunisia and the island of Pantelleria as E-boat packs struck, putting yet another cruiser out of the battle and sinking four merchantmen.

Service Squabble. By six a.m., the tanker had caught up with the remnants of the convoy—in time to face the consequence of Axis decisions taken overnight in Rome. Despite heavy losses, German and Italian air chiefs in Rome were determined that their bombers should finish Operation Pedestal, arguing with naval commanders over which service should get the fighter cover. Asked to adjudicate, Mussolini favoured the bombers, even though an overwhelmingly strong Italian fleet was already on its way to complete the massacre. At midnight, the fleet was recalled—"a more useless waste of fighting power cannot be imagined," records a German admiral—and at eight a.m. on August 13, the bombers found their quarry once more.

Last in line because of her defective steering, *Ohio* was the main target, but first hit was the convoy's largest vessel, the 12,843-ton SS *Waimarama,* 600 yards ahead of her. The effect was cataclysmic. Carrying aviation fuel and ammunition, *Waimarama* disintegrated in an explosion so violent that one bomber was blasted out of the sky. For half a mile, the petrol-covered sea blazed, jetting flame up to 2,000 feet.

Steering Clear. *Ohio* could not hope to survive if the fire reached her oozing port-side wound. "Hard-a-port!" thundered Mason on the phone. Gray slammed over the helm. Still they headed for the crimson wall of fire. Praying that *Ohio* would respond, Gray battled with the wheel. Slowly the high bow swung away, and the tanker's starboard side skirted the inferno.

Miraculously spared one disaster, *Ohio* was almost immediately seesawing violently from the force of a bomb that burst under her bow. Calling for a damage report, Mason was told, "There's water in the forepeak." The extra burden forced the tanker to steam bow down, heightening the strain on her already perilously weakened hull.

Bill McConalogue and his brother John, another *Ohio* greaser, decided that the chances of both of them surviving were now slender. Devoted family men, they made a pact: if one came through, he would do his utmost to support the other's family.

By now the forecastle gun was out of action, but *Ohio's* other guns were seldom silent. Around 9.30 a.m. they shattered a Stuka that crashed into the ship's side, showering wreckage on the poop. One large section dropped eight feet from Gray, who grinned at Third Officer Jock Stephen. "This will cheer the Old Man up. Give him my compliments and tell him what's happened."

Stephen came off the phone looking dazed. "The Old Man says that's nothing—they've had a Ju-88 on the foredeck for some time."

Incredibly, within minutes, *Ohio's* gun crews had brought down two German bombers. When the first loomed 15 feet in front of the bridge, Mason saw only a hurtling blur. As the aircraft hit the deck, its engine was wrenched from the fuselage and hurled overboard —providentially, for its red-hot manifolds would have ignited the fuel from the bomber's tanks.

Fresh waves of bombers took up

the attack. They swooped on *Ohio*, dropping sticks of bombs that exploded simultaneously on either side of the ship. Around 20,000 tons deadweight were lifted something like 30 feet out of the water—so cleanly that a crew member of a near-by destroyer claimed he saw daylight below the full length of *Ohio's* keel. As she dropped back again, vibrating violently, walls of green water rose high all about her. It seemed that her weakened hull must break in two. But she shook off the deluge, kept her battered bow towards Malta and steamed on.

From Mason's log: "Enemy planes are continually bombing. Gunners and crew keeping up a deadly and accurate barrage."

After 30 minutes a bomb fell near enough to cut the fuel supply and stop the engines. In the hot sticky darkness under the boilers, Wyld and another engineer groped through the complex network of pipes so that they could again raise steam. But after two further explosions in the furnace, Wyld reported to the bridge: "The boilers are completely out of action. We can't proceed under our own steam."

Ohio was 80 miles from Malta and her best bet now was to continue under tow, hitched to a destroyer. To replace the useless steering engine, Gray, Stephen and four crewmen rigged chain blocks to the top of the five-ton rudder. But the destroyer could get little way on and *Ohio* turned in circles until the towline parted.

The arrival of a minesweeper and two launches from Malta failed to provide sufficient power to tow *Ohio*. Finally, when a bomb wrecked the tanker's engine room and crew quarters, Mason ordered his men to spend the night less vulnerably aboard the naval vessels.

As Bill McConalogue was about to leave the ship, he could see nothing of his brother John. "Are you sure everyone's off?" he asked the Chief Engineer. Wyld went back to search the accommodation, now blindingly fogged with asbestos dust from shattered steam-pipe lagging, but he found no one. Believing his brother to be dead, McConalogue silently renewed his vow: John's family was now his responsibility.

Taking Stock. For Mason, the next morning—August 14—was sombre. Overnight one of the launches had vanished, and with it 30 of his crew, including most of his officers and engineers. In the first raids of the day, bombs carried away *Ohio's* rudder and worsened damage aft. The one source of hope was the arrival of another destroyer, improving prospects of a tow—if *Ohio* could be kept afloat.

Surveying his ship, Mason found that the stern was settling deep in the water and the main deck was so badly buckled that, seen from aft, the masts had taken the shape of a letter V. "But she'll last another 12 hours," Mason told the senior naval

The damaged tanker SS Ohio, supported by Royal Navy destroyers, approaches Malta

officer. "It can be done. It must be done."

With three destroyers as tugs—the pumps from one keeping water from rising at more than six inches an hour in *Ohio's* engine room—the voyage resumed at five knots and, as Mason's log commented laconically, "under the most difficult conditions owing to air activity." But *Ohio's* guns helped to shoot down a third aircraft, before she crept into Valetta's Grand Harbour at eight a.m. on August 15.

Crowds swarmed the high ramparts. In their churches they had joined in a novena—nine days of special prayer—that Malta might be relieved. Now, as they stared down incredulously, it seemed that the prayers had been answered. For only a miracle could have brought to journey's end this battered hulk so near sinking that a man could reach down from the main deck and touch the water.

Of the 14 merchantmen in Operation Pedestal, nine, carrying 85,000 tons of cargo, had been lost. Last of the five that had won through, with 55,000 tons of supplies, was *Ohio*.

"The reward justified the price exacted," Winston Churchill wrote in *The Second World War*. "Revictualled and replenished with ammunition and vital stores, the strength of Malta revived, British submarines returned to the island, and, with the striking forces of the RAF, regained their dominating position in the Central Mediterranean."

As *Ohio* moved slowly to her berth, the indomitable Mason still slimly erect on his battered bridge, cheers thundered from the ramparts and the band played *Rule, Britannia*. Watching from the quayside with special pride were 30 men—the involuntarily missing crew members who had arrived the previous day in a launch that had withdrawn from the battle because of engine trouble. Among them was Bill McConalogue, who spotted his brother John on *Ohio's* deck. Seamanlike, their greeting was brief.

"So you made it."

"Yes, thank God."

Four months before, King George VI had uniquely recognized Malta's courage with the George Cross. Now he made this same award to Captain Mason, the first Merchant Navy officer to receive the supreme decoration for civilian gallantry.

In all, 14 members of *Ohio's* crew were given awards—Gray, Stephen, Wyld and others. Never before had there been such a voyage as that of SS *Ohio* to Malta.

Bugging the Line

WHEN my five-year-old had a high temperature, the doctor arrived and examined his chest with a stethoscope. "Doctor, are you phoning the germs?" asked the boy.

—Jean Charles, *Il Riso in Erba*

HUMOUR in Uniform

THE MAJOR at our Cadet Camp was a reckless driver who scared us to death every time he took a lorry-load of us down the main road. Finally one of our lads hit on a tactful way of restraining our dare-devil commanding officer. With a tin of black paint he added two commas to the traffic sign outside the camp so that it read : "Halt, major, road ahead."

—I. M. SMALL, Hornchurch, Essex

WHILE I was serving in a destroyer my duties took me to the bridge one evening. The captain was taking a celestial bearing, commonly called "shooting the stars."

As he did so, a falling star blazed a trail across the sky. A seaman standing near by exclaimed, "Good Heavens, the commander finally hit one!"

—A. G. MURPHY

OUR AIRSTRIP in Italy during the war was next to an olive grove. At harvest time, young boys and women spread canvas beneath the trees and struck the branches with long sticks to knock the olives on to the canvas. One enterprising pilot, after observing this slow technique that had been handed down from generation to generation, decided to go into the olive-picking business himself and offered to pick the entire orchard for two live chickens. The next day, returning from a mission, he made several low passes over the trees. The backwash from his fighter shook every olive on to the canvas.

—C. FREEMAN

To KILL time on the Sarawak border in 1963, my mate amused himself by writing appreciatively to the manufacturers of small but desirable products—toilet articles, sweets, stationery. The result was a rich haul of items sent with the compliments of the flattered firms.

He met his match, however, when he wrote to Wilkinson Sword about their stainless-steel razor blades. "I have used one of your excellent blades for three months continuously while patrolling the jungles of Sarawak and

often shaving in cold water," he told them.

In due course came their reply : "Thank you for your complimentary remarks about our product. Please find a further three months' supply enclosed." With the letter came a single blade.—SGT. D. BLEVINS, R.M., 45 Commando Royal Marines, B.F.P.O. 69

Untold Stories of D-Day

By Cornelius Ryan

The momentous events of June 6, 1944 are
remembered now with pride, nostalgia
and a kind of reverence. Individual experiences
make this day synonymous with courage

C. E. TURNER/ILLUSTRATED LONDON NEWS

WHEN I completed *The Longest Day* in 1959, I thought I had little more to say. To detail the awesome 24 hours of that historic invasion of a coastline Hitler claimed to be impregnable, I had leafed through volumes of research, read everything I could unearth on the subject and, with Reader's Digest editors and researchers, contacted or interviewed German and Allied D-Day veterans all over the world. But I soon discovered there was no end

to the longest day. The book triggered an avalanche of mail—some 20,000 letters over the years—which has not ceased even now.

Written in various languages, many of the letters are anguished or pathetic. In particular, there are those from German families seeking information on the fate of a son, husband or other relative. The sister of Lieutenant-Colonel Hellmuth Meyer, the German intelligence officer who discovered the invasion date by deciphering a message intended for the French resistance, learned from *The Longest Day* that he was alive, and brother and sister were eventually reunited.

Perhaps the most heart-warming letter I ever received came from the daughter of a D-Day veteran. In 1970, she wrote: "I am 27, and I never knew my father. He was killed on Omaha Beach. For years I hated him because I was tired of Mother talking about the war and what a hero my father was." Then, reading about Omaha Beach, she found her attitude changed.

"My father became real to me," she continued. "I cried because I love him and he might have loved me. I cried too because his life was over before mine ever really began, yet he gave me my life. Thank you for giving me my father after all these years." That letter alone made

Based on eye-witness observations, this painting shows the establishment of the first beach-head on Normandy's shores

the ten years of work on *The Longest Day* totally worthwhile.

One of the more intriguing aspects of the mail I receive is the revelation of material I did not have when I was writing the book. My favourite "new" fact deals with the historically minded Winston Churchill. Early in 1944, he called a meeting of the Supreme Commander, General Dwight D. Eisenhower, and his D-Day officers to discuss the date of the attack. After dinner at the Prime Minister's country house, Chequers in Buckinghamshire, Churchill sipped at a brandy. Leaning forward, he asked, "Gentlemen, when do we go?"

The importance of weather was explained to Churchill, and he was assured the invasion would take place towards the end of spring or early summer. The late Rear-Admiral Alan Kirk, who was to command the Omaha and Utah beach naval task forces, was struck by the Prime Minister's expression. He looked, Kirk thought, like "a mild but somewhat exasperated

---

DUBLIN-BORN Cornelius Ryan, 54, became a Fleet Street war correspondent in 1943. He flew on 14 bombing raids, covered the D-Day landing and the Allied drive across France and Germany. In 1945, he went to the Far East, where he reported the end of hostilities and the Bikini A-bomb tests.

Following *The Longest Day* and *The Last Battle*, a re-creation of the Fall of Berlin, he will complete his trilogy on the Second World War in Europe with *A Bridge Too Far*, to be published in September (Hamish Hamilton at £3·95) marking the thirtieth anniversary of the Battle of Arnhem.

bulldog." Gazing at each of the D-Day commanders, Churchill rumbled: "Pray tell me, gentlemen, when did William go?"

There was a long, embarrassed silence. Recalls Kirk: "Here we sat, the D-Day generals and admirals of the United States and Great Britain, the products of our respective nations' proud naval and military academies, men who had studied every conceivable problem of the invasion, and not one of us remembered what time of year William the Conqueror, sailing from Normandy, had landed in England."

Conquering Heroes. When *had* William landed? Churchill knew that it was not in the spring or summer, but in the autumn. He came ashore at the little fishing village of Pevensey, Sussex, on September 28, 1066. Another intriguing fact of William's conquest had not escaped Churchill. He explained that William had assembled his ships at the mouth of the Dives and sailed from the Bay of the Seine—the precise area where the Allied armies were to invade almost 900 years later. Had the Germans thought of this historical coincidence? Luckily not.

What was the German Supreme Commander, Field-Marshal Gerd von Rundstedt, doing on the morning of D-Day? The gardener employed at the villa next to von Rundstedt's supplied the information in a letter: von Rundstedt was working in his rose garden. By coincidence, so was the D-Day Allied commander, Field-Marshal Bernard Law Montgomery. "There was nothing else for me to do," Montgomery explained, "but wait for news of the landings."

As midnight of June 5 approached, great trains of paratroop aircraft and infantry-filled gliders towed by DC-3's approached the Normandy coast. Courage and fear rode in every plane. Some paratroopers— like Private Bill Dunnett of the 1st Canadian Parachute Battalion— were so calm that they fell asleep almost before their planes left the ground. Dunnett remembered nothing until he was awakened by the man next to him and, seconds later, was out of the door and floating down on Normandy. He thought it was "a hell of a way to wake up— without even a cup of tea."

Take-Off. Sergeant John McCallion May of the British 6th Airborne remembered the pilot's remarks about his plane. "She's rather delicate, so don't move about too much." May spent the entire trip worrying about the plane. And Private Stanley Fortnam fretted about what it would be like to force-land in the English Channel.

Nearing their drop zones, everyone from generals to privates seems to have been fascinated by the moonlit, peaceful-looking landscape over Normandy. America's General James Gavin of the 82nd Airborne mentally noted that "there was no evidence of human habitation . . . no people or vehicles . . . brown-red countryside traced through by neat white roads . . . off to the right, large amounts of flak . . . quite beautiful as it arched up in high and low bursts."

As the first soldiers jumped into the night sky, their parachutes blossoming above them, there was little time to speculate on what lay ahead. As Sergeant May put it: "Everyone was afraid of appearing afraid, and that's what courage really is—not letting the other fellow know how scared you really are."

As one officer stood by the door of his plane ready to jump, he issued a final order that Sergeant John Faor remembers only too well. "Now listen," the officer yelled. "Anyone—and I mean anyone—who breaks a leg on this darn jump gets a court martial! Got it? OK, let's go." Minutes later, Faor was lying in an apple orchard —with a broken leg. The officer, who landed near by, was "cursing his head off." He had broken an ankle.

As paratroopers fought in the darkness of the Normandy hedgerows, the great D-Day armada steamed across the Channel. Convoy after convoy—from motor-torpedo boats to supply-laden tramp steamers to troop transports to battleships—ploughed through the wind-chopped seas in what must surely go down in naval history as the greatest logistical shipping movement ever attempted. The output of naval orders alone called for several thousand workers. Each vessel was given a numbered position in its convoy, travelled at a certain speed, and upon arrival in the Bay of the Seine rode at anchor according to a master plan—all without breaking radio silence. The wonder is that there were no collisions and that the huge fleet was not detected.

Of the many stories that have come to light since *The Longest Day* was written, a unique incident stands out. In the gigantic 5,000-vessel fleet operation, all but one ship crossed the Channel. Anchored off Spithead, the old Indian liner *Neutralia* should have sailed on the evening of June 5. British 7th Armoured Division troops on her decks cheered and waved as other ships moved out. Gradually the cheering ceased. Army officers aboard protested to *Neutralia's* skipper that something had gone wrong —but he had received no orders and could not move without them.

What had happened? Through an oversight, naval orders for *Neutralia* were never issued. In fact, the absence of *Neutralia's* troops was not even noticed until five days after D-Day. A search was made for the "lost" transport, and she was discovered still at anchor—along with her cargo of frustrated troops.

As dawn broke on D-Day, the majestic Allied armada lined up across the horizon was an unforgettable sight. On the bridge of USS *Bayfield,* flagship for all the naval forces off Utah Beach, Commander John Moreno, assistant planning officer, gazed through his binoculars. One ship intrigued him. Her name remains a mystery but, says Moreno, "she had been built solely to bombard German shore installations in the First World War but was never used."

As *Bayfield* moved slowly past, Moreno saw the British gunboat break open her colours. "A storm of bunting appeared," Moreno recalls, "spelling out Nelson's famous message to the fleet at Trafalgar: 'England Expects Every Man to Do His Duty.'" Then with a thunderous roar, the gunboat's two massive 15-inchers opened fire, but only once. They failed to retract, and she couldn't fire again. As she was towed slowly out of the firing line, men lined the rails of other ships to cheer her. Her moment of destiny had come and gone—but it was not forgotten.

The ships poured millions of pounds of high explosives into the German coastal defences. The US destroyer *Satterlee* lay so close off rocky Pointe du Hoc that many thought she would founder. She moved to and fro all morning, guns firing point-blank to aid US Rangers as they fought up the nine-storey-high cliffs to silence guns that they soon discovered had never been installed.

As troops began to wade ashore

ROGER-VIOLLET/REX FEATURES

British soldiers landing on the beach in Normandy

beneath the bombardment's umbrella, there were incidents of horror, heroism—and even humour. On Omaha Beach, where 2,000 Americans became casualties in just three hours, General Harold Blakeley of the US 4th Division was struck by the coolness of his British liaison officer. As they sloshed ashore, Blakeley asked, "How many beaches will this make for you?" A shell burst near by. Without pausing, his companion said, "Seven landings, sir—that is, if you allow me to count Dunkirk."

Scores of men remember one particular sight. At the height of the battle on Omaha Beach, a middle-aged French civilian appeared with his son. "They had enough courage for 50 of us," recalls Major Elmore Swenson. "As we lay pinned down, we saw them, surrounded by small-arms fire, calmly rowing a boat back and forth picking up the dead, dying and wounded from the water. Who they were or where they came from we never found out."

Some wounded men on Omaha Beach thought that they were delirious when in the water off Pointe du Hoc they spotted what appeared to be red fire ladders waving high in the air. They *were* fire ladders. Borrowed from the London Fire Brigade, they had been mounted in landing craft and from their 100-foot-high tops US Rangers were pouring machine-gun fire at Germans on the cliffs.

Each beach had its own share of stories. One of the more poignant occurred on Sword Beach. As Commander Philippe Kieffer led his French commandos ashore under a storm of fire, a commando fell fatally wounded next to Kieffer. Dragging the man on to the beach, Kieffer saw that he wore an old First World War French helmet. "It was my father's," the soldier said. "He wore it at Verdun."

As Kieffer lowered the man to the beach, the commando spoke once more: "One favour. Before you go, turn my head towards Paris."

Year after year, new information reaches me about D-Day. From all sources one belief is expressed again and again: people everywhere identify with and believe in the overwhelming courage shown that day. Many of them have quoted the words of the sergeant who told his frightened squad before the invasion: "Remember this. If you get it, the remainder of us will say of you: it was a good way to die, on the beaches of Normandy."

Out in the Code

ANSWERING his phone, a friend was asked: "Can I speak to Sid?" "No Sid here," he replied.

There was a pause, then the caller said, "Sorry, I must have dialled his VAT number."

—PHS in *The Times*

The Pied Piper
of 'A' Company

BY JEROME KELLEY

M Y STORY begins in a Marine Corps recruiting office
in Montpelier, Vermont,
USA, a few days after Pearl Harbour.
The square-jawed recruiting
sergeant sat behind his scarred,
wooden desk, tapping with his pencil as he looked me up and down.

When he finally spoke, the tapping
cadence seemed to underline every
word: "Kelley, the Marine Corps is
turning you down. For a start, you're
only 17 and you haven't got your
parents' consent. Secondly, you're
underweight. Thirdly, you have
the *flattest* feet the doctor has ever

seen!" And he started to laugh.

That did it. "Let me tell *you* something!" I exploded. "You'll still be a recruiting sergeant in Montpelier when I'm overseas with a fighting outfit!"

"Oh, ho!" he chuckled. "I'll bet you a month's pay on *that*."

That night I ran away from home. And the following day, lying about my age, I enlisted in the Canadian Army in Montreal.

Tenderfoot. The weeks of infantry training in Quebec weren't too tough. And life at the replacement depot in the south of England was even softer. Mostly we played cards or walked round the countryside. Then came the day of reckoning—posting to our regular units. The driver dropped me off in front of a row of decrepit houses on a desolate stretch of the Sussex coast.

"Well, good luck," he said cheerfully. "They claim this is the toughest unit in the Canadian Army." He waved merrily as he drove off.

I heaved my bag on to my shoulder and staggered towards a building marked "HQ 'A' Company, 1st Battalion, Black Watch of Canada." Inside, a craggy-faced sergeant-major briefly studied my records, then, leaving me standing stiffly to attention, departed through a door to his right.

"Sir," I heard him say, "we've just received a replacement."

"A replacement! We indent for eight replacements and they send us *one*. What is he—Superman?"

"Hardly, sir. He weighs nine stone and has barely a whisker. He'll be the smallest lad in the company. Also, sir, he's flat-footed."

I heard a snort. "Post him to Lieutenant Dorrance's platoon and inform the lieutenant that the new replacement will go with the rest of the company on the Kingley Bottom exercise this afternoon."

Two hours later, in full marching order with 60-pound packs, 'A' Company fell in. Whatever lay in store for us wasn't exciting much joy in the ranks. "Here we go again, fifth exercise in six weeks!" . . . "Wonder why he missed a week?" . . . "Third time my leave's been cancelled." . . . "Kingley Bottom?" . . . "Yes, the Valley of Death!" . . . "I should have joined the navy . . ."

"Ten-*shun!*" an officer barked.

The barrel-chested company commander, Major Philip Griffin, marched up and down in front of the company for three solid minutes before he spoke. "It's come to my attention that many of you think these exercises are unnecessary. You're wrong! Soon you will meet the German Army in combat. The toughest, best-trained troops will win and suffer the fewest casualties. Therefore, whether you like it or not, *you* are going to be the toughest, best-trained company in the Canadian Army. It's as simple as that!"

The major positioned himself directly in front of me. "Just one more thing!" he yelled, his piercing eyes sizing me up. "Since this company went on active service in 1939, no member has ever fallen out of a line of march. That record will not — repeat, will *not* — be blemished!"

With no further ceremony, 'A' Company marched off behind its two bagpipers and single drummer, to the tune of "Scotland the Brave."

The torturous nine-hour march to Kingley Bottom was the prelude to five days of sheer, uninterrupted misery. It was night attack, advance, withdrawal, night patrol, platoon attacks, company attacks, firing, guard duty, poor food, cold food, no food, infiltration, wire cutting, demolition, river crossings. And rain. Four days of cold, bone-chilling rain. During all this time no one spoke to me except to issue an order.

Bleak Outlook. On the night before the return march I was huddled under my poncho, wet, muddy and shivering. Tomorrow would be my eighteenth birthday. I kept thinking of my family in Montpelier, and of the birthday cakes my mother used to bake. For once I was glad it was raining. The rain camouflaged my tears.

"Mind if I draw up a chunk of mud and sit?" someone asked. It was Keay, one of the company's bagpipers. "How's it going?"

For the next hour I unburdened myself to Piper Keay. I told him about being an American, about the Marine sergeant in Vermont, about

running away and lying about my age, and how tomorrow would be my eighteenth birthday. Finally I said, "I'm scared!"

"Scared of what?"

"Scared that tomorrow I'm going to be the first member of 'A' Company ever to fall out of a line of march."

Relief Orders. I told him of the running sores on my shoulders caused by my web equipment, and how the broken blisters on my feet had become infected. He thought for a moment. "Those your blankets?" He pointed to the sodden pile. I nodded. He picked them up. "Stay put," he said. "I'll be back."

He returned carrying a poncho-wrapped bundle and his medical kit. In those days, pipers and drummers doubled as medical assistants. "Take off your boots and socks," he ordered as he rammed a thermometer into my mouth. Reading the thermometer by torch, he clucked, shook three tablets out of a bottle and growled, "Swallow 'em!" Next, he disinfected and bandaged my raw feet. "Here, put on these dry socks."

"Where did you get dry socks?"

"Same place as I got dry blankets," he said, nodding to the poncho-wrapped bundle. "The Quartermaster-Sergeant likes a tot of medicinal rum once in a while. Now, let's get those sores on your shoulders treated."

In the breakfast queue next morning, Piper Keay was behind me, a bright smile creasing his leathery face. "Still scared?" he asked.

"Yes!"

"Well, you're going to make this march, because Piper Keay is going to make certain you do!"

Fifty minutes marching, ten-minute halt; 50 minutes marching, ten-minute halt. The miles fell away as tired, muddy 'A' Company plodded homewards. After the third hour my feet began to bleed. Sergeant McCallum, my platoon sergeant, fell in beside me. "Feet bleeding, Kelley?"

"Yes, sergeant."

"Piper Keay expected they would. At the next halt take off your boots and Keay will fix you up. Meanwhile, I want you to know you're doing a good job."

The kind words from the sergeant were like medicine. At the next halt Keay rebandaged my feet. Then he handed me a small bottle. "Drink this!"

I forced down the contents and started to choke. "What's that?"

"Your birthday drink. Some rum the QM-sergeant didn't get last night. It'll keep you going for another hour."

During the next 50 minutes, when he wasn't playing his pipes, Keay seemed to be all over the line of march. I saw him speak to Lieutenant Dorrance, then to a big private named Berry and, finally, to the sergeant-major. The sergeant-major moved up alongside Major Griffin. They talked a moment.

The major nodded his head and actually smiled.

The next segment of the march was one I dreaded. It was my turn to carry the 22-pound Bren gun. During the halt I went forward to get it from Berry. He eyed me up and down. "It's my turn to carry the Bren," I said.

"It's your birthday, ain't it?"

"Yes, but . . ."

"But what? For a birthday present the section's decided you can miss your turn."

I started to protest. "Shut up!" Berry snarled. Then he smiled. "And happy birthday!"

As we drew abreast of Chichester's market cross, there was a loud flourish on the drum and then the skirling of pipes. I heard it, but I didn't believe it. The pipes were playing "Happy Birthday"! Lieutenant Dorrance gave me a pat on the back. "Happy birthday, Kelley! Only five more miles to go."

"Do or Die." They say the last mile is the hardest. I'm a believer. By the time we came in sight of our billets, blood was oozing out of my boots and was running down both arms from my lacerated shoulders. Spots shimmered in front of my eyes, and I was staggering. *Keep going. One more step. Don't fall.* I kept repeating these words over and over to myself. Then I heard the pipes again. They were playing a tune that, I'm certain, bagpipes had never played before, and it carried me those last, painful steps. The melody was ragged but unmistakable. They were playing "Yankee Doodle."

When the command "Dismissed" was given, I slumped to the ground. Suddenly a form loomed over me. "Kelley!" I recognized the voice as Major Griffin's and tried to get to my feet. "As you were!" A hand reached down and gripped one of mine. "Happy birthday, Kelley. Show the guts you've shown today and one day you'll have your commission."

Two YEARS later, the major's prediction came true. I was sent to officers' training school in Canada and received my commission. One day, while on leave in Montpelier before re-embarkation, I spotted my old friend, the Marine recruiting sergeant, coming towards me. Even from a distance I could see him eyeing me curiously. Watching his face

was like watching a kaleidoscope. Recognition, surprise, amazement and disbelief flashed over it. A few paces from me he snapped the smartest salute I'd ever received. I returned it and let him pass before I barked, "Sergeant!"

He wheeled about. "Sir?"

"Sergeant," I said, "my name is Kelley. I wonder if you happen to have a month's pay on you."

"Kelley? Oh, ah, er, yes, sir! There was a bet, wasn't there, sir?"

"Right, sergeant. But let's forget it. I got over being mad at the Marine Corps years ago. As a matter of fact, I'd like to give you Marines a suggestion that might hasten the end of the war. You ought to recruit bagpipers. A good bagpiper can make a soldier out of an under-aged, underweight, flat-footed recruit overnight."

I left the good sergeant standing in the middle of the street, looking perplexed.

Quotable Quotes

ANYBODY can be a heart specialist. The only requirement is loving somebody. —A. P.

I DON'T believe in the generation gap. I believe in *re*generation gaps. Each day you regenerate—or else you're not living. —Duke Ellington

LISTENING to both sides of a story will convince you that there is more to a story than both sides. —F. T.

YOU never realize what a good memory you have until you try to forget something. —F. P. J.

THERE is no truth existing which I fear, or would wish unknown to the whole world. —Thomas Jefferson

'We Were the World's First Skyjackers'

By Squadron Leader W. M. Dunsmore, DFC
as told to George Pollock

Every time I read that a plane has been seized in mid-air, I wonder what Ted Strever, Ray Brown and John (Wilkie) Wilkinson make of it. The four of us were the world's first skyjackers—a word then still to be invented—but in circumstances very different from today's aerial take-overs.

It was 1942. Hitler's Afrika Korps were sweeping triumphantly across the sands of Libya, and the job of our No. 217 Squadron of the RAF was to help sink as many of their supply ships as possible. On July 28 we took off from Malta in our Beaufort torpedo-bomber, but while successfully torpedoing a 10,000-ton Axis freighter, we had been hit and forced down, then rescued from our rubber dinghy by an Italian seaplane and taken as prisoners of war to a

small Italian Air Force base on the Greek island of Levkas.

Now, the following morning, we were in another Italian seaplane, flying at 2,500 feet above the sun-drenched Ionian Sea. Our destination: the huge Italian naval base at Taranto, on the "instep" of Italy, 250 miles away. Our fate: interrogation, followed by maybe years behind barbed wire.

"I don't like the sound of Taranto," muttered a voice in my ear. None of us did. Our average age was around 24, and collectively we could exert a fair amount of youthful punch. Ted Strever, our South African skipper, was six feet three inches tall and as strong as they come. Ray Brown and Wilkie Wilkinson, our wireless operator/air gunners, were sturdy New Zealanders. I, the British member of the crew and navigator, could make up for any weight the others might lack. But our RAF escape drill, which made clear our duty to attempt to escape if captured, hadn't prepared us for this particular situation.

Tight Spot. Not only were we huddled in a sunken compartment, tiny and windowless, at the rear of the plane, we were also under armed guard. In addition to the crew of four, the seaplane—a triple-engined Cant—carried an extra man: a soldier wearing on his hip an enormous, long-barrelled revolver.

He stood at the top of a high step rising out of our compartment, blocking the narrow passage along the right-hand side of the fuselage to the front of the plane. Up front sat the captain, with the engineer to his right. Behind the captain sat the second pilot and then the wireless operator, whose desk was against the fuselage, on the level above our compartment and opposite the guard.

The plane droned on. As far as we could make out, only the guard had a gun. We exchanged glances, wondering how we could get it from him.

Studying the guard, we realized that his attention was entirely taken by his view from a window. It was, we discovered later, his first flight, and never before had he seen anything like the panorama of sea that shimmered beneath the aircraft. He seemed hypnotized by it. The wireless operator appeared equally engrossed with work at his desk.

Acting entirely on his own initiative, Wilkie made the first move. He stood up, tapped the wireless operator on the shoulder and pointed dramatically out of the window. Startled, the Italian looked up.

Instantly, Wilkie blurred into action. His right fist caught the wireless operator's jaw. As the man sagged, Wilkie yanked him from his seat and the rest of us pinned him to the floor. Before the guard could recover from his entranced state induced by the view, Wilkie whipped the big revolver from his holster and

ILLUSTRATION: NEVILLE DEAR

shouted, "Here you are, Ted!"

The guard let out a wail and collapsed on top of the second pilot. Wilkie reached out and hauled the guard into captivity; as he did so, he saw the captain turn and rise from his seat up front. Wilkie knew then that we had been wrong in thinking that only the guard was armed. The captain held an automatic pistol, its blunt snout directed at him.

Immediately, though, Ted countered, pointing the big revolver at the captain. The first to get in a shot would be the victor.

Turning Point. But the balance of power was upset by the engineer. To see what was happening aft, he had left his seat and now stood beside the captain. Realizing that if shooting started in such a confined space he might well stop a bullet, he lunged to his right. He fell against the captain, inadvertently knocking the automatic from his hand.

It was over. The Cant was ours.

Ray and I took the captain and the engineer into captivity in the rear compartment along with the guard and wireless operator. We tied their wrists with belts to prevent their attempting a reverse skyjacking. Then I went forward. Wilkie was covering the second pilot and Ted was in the captain's seat flying the Cant.

I searched the aircraft for maps but there was none on board. At least the compass was standard. So once we knew where we were, I could set a course. I sketched a map

of the heel and foot of Italy, Sicily and Malta.

"What we've got to do," I said, "is fly due west till we hit Italy, coast-crawl down till we hit Sicily, then strike south for Malta."

We reckoned the distance at well over 300 miles.

Our trussed prisoners aft were far from happy. We discovered that they had been taking us to Taranto only because they happened to be flying there on leave. Unhappiest of all was the guard, who now had acute first-flight nerves and any moment was going to be air-sick. I felt sorry for him. We had no personal animosity for these enemies of ours, whose fellow Italians on Levkas had wined and dined us royally.

I decided to free the guard and let him recover. The captain couldn't see why the man responsible for their troubles should get preferential treatment. So I untied him, too, hoping he might help me to improve my map.

I showed it to him. He studied it, made several alterations, then, curious to know our destination, wrote on it, "Africa?"

Crossing that out, I wrote, "Malta."

He stared at me in horror. Snatching back the map, he wrote: "Spitfires—Hurricanes!"

"San-fairy-ann," I shrugged.

The next Italian to become agitated was the engineer. He shouted: *"Benzina, benzina!"*

The fuel tank was running dry.

None of us had the faintest notion where the reserve fuel switch might be, so we untied the engineer and sent him forward to his control panel. Just in time, he switched on the reserve supply.

With one Italian still in the second pilot's seat and three others now freed, it seemed churlish to keep the wireless operator tethered, so we untied him as well.

Flight Path. A thin line appeared on the horizon: the Italian coast. Since we couldn't risk getting too close to it, we flew south for about 20 minutes, turned west until we sighted it again, then repeated the manoeuvre. Thus, in a series of steps, we worked our way down the foot of Italy.

Wilkie and Ray decided against even trying to operate the radio, to let Malta flying control know what was happening, in case this enabled the enemy to fix our position. We would have to risk an unannounced approach to the best-defended island in the Mediterranean.

Suddenly Wilkie shouted, "Ju-52!"

The Nazi aircraft was coming up on us fast from behind. As it closed in on us, Ray climbed into the rear gun position and wagged the Cant's guns up and down in the recognized RAF "friendly aircraft" signal. To our relief, it worked. The Ju-52 turned north and vanished.

Soon after this encounter we reached the southern tip of Italy, crossed the Strait of Messina and flew in steps down the east coast of Sicily until we reached the most southerly point, Cape Passero. Only some 60 miles separated us from Malta.

There was now real doubt, though, that we could make it. The engineer sounded the warning. Pointing to the fuel gauges, he inscribed an arc on the face of his wristwatch. His meaning was clear. We had barely enough *benzina* for half an hour's flying: perhaps 60 miles, perhaps not.

Eventually we sighted land. Lacking the fuel to make good any error, we had to be sure this was Malta. None of us had seen the island's north coast before because we always took off and landed in the south to avoid the German radar covering the island from Sicily. To be absolutely certain we had reached our right destination we had to get close enough to spot a clinching landmark. By then, of course, RAF radar would have spotted us.

"This," said Wilkie, "is when we could do with knowing how to work the radio."

Aerobatics. We prepared for the attack. To have the most experienced man at the controls, Ted motioned the Italian captain to take over. Then, backing his words with graphic gestures, he said, "When we shout, put the plane down."

We now all peered towards the rapidly approaching land. Suddenly we spotted a cluster of tall radio masts which we identified as those on the hill behind Valletta, Malta's capital. At least, my makeshift navigation had proved sound.

At that moment, from the upper gun position, Ray shouted: "Spitfires! Spits!"

Four of them in line astern roared down to attack. "Down, down, down!" bellowed Ted. The Cant's nose dipped sharply towards the sea. Within seconds we heard the sharp staccato of machine-guns, the screech of ripping metal, then the heavier explosion of cannon followed by the thump of shells juddering into our plane.

The floats parted the water into sheets of spray. The engines cut, whether switched off by the captain or because the tanks were dry we didn't know. I whipped off my shirt and vest—the only white article I had—and waved it out of the window. The Spitfires needed to be in no doubt we had "surrendered."

Leaving one as sentinel, the fighters returned to base, and we had time to count the holes in the Cant: 20 machine-gun bullets and eight cannon shells had torn into the wings. We were grateful to the Spitfire boys for having spared our fuselage. With nine of us packed into it, they could not have missed us. The world's first skyjacking was over — six years before the "first hijacking" recorded in *The Shell Book of Firsts.*

From the shore two miles away, a rescue launch appeared, the crew crouched at their guns. But as they drew alongside, they goggled in disbelief. "You're RAF?" gasped one. "Blimey, we thought it was old Mussolini coming to give himself up!"

Happy Landing. We, of course, were jubilant; the Italians were philosophical. They took bottles of wine from their leave cases, and we all drank to each other as the launch towed us into St. Paul's Bay.

Although the Italians could not receive hospitality such as we had enjoyed on Levkas — beleaguered Malta was too close to starvation— we requested every possible privilege for them while awaiting transfer to prison camps in Britain. It was the least we could do for men whose leave, and freedom, we had interrupted until the war was over.

For us there was celebration. Ted and I received immediate awards of the DFC, Wilkie and Ray the DFM —the only time the RAF has ever had reason to decorate skyjackers.

I had to wait until October 1945 to learn how the Italians felt about it all. Then from a prison camp at Belper in Derbyshire I received a letter from the Cant's skipper. Written in the friendliest terms, it concluded: "I do hope you are well." I'll wager that none of today's skyjackers ever receives such a letter from his victims.

Love is a glass which shatters if you hold it too tightly or too loosely.
—Russian proverb

Victorious in two
World Wars, he also won
the hearts of his
men, and of the nation

WINSTON Churchill thought
him a Cromwellian
figure—"austere, severe,
accomplished, tireless, his life
given to the study of war." His
countrymen knew him simply as
"Monty," the cocky little commander who at El Alamein in the North
African desert in 1942 had won the
victory which symbolized for the
free world the turning point of
the Second World War.

In Europe, where he later led the
Allied armies, they called Field
Marshal Montgomery "The Libera-
tor," but Monty didn't look the part.
Five feet eight, lean and briskly

Monty,
the People's General

By Peter Browne

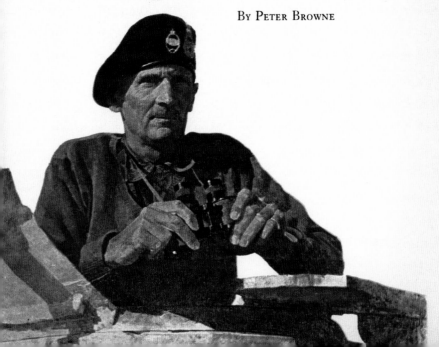

alert, he reminded one of his generals of an intelligent terrier which might bite at any moment. It was the piercing eyes that men noticed most. Said George Bernard Shaw, "Like a burning glass, he concentrates all space into a single spot."

Monty bristled with confidence. He had such an immense belief in his own ability, it was said that while to serve under him was a privilege, to serve over him was hell. He was one of the few men who would brook no interference from Churchill. "Prime Minister," he once snapped, "you are not a professional soldier. I am. You do not know how to fight this battle. I do."

Spartan Existence. Legend painted him as a puritan—teetotal, non-smoking, monastic in his way of life. Even Churchill contributed to the image of his asceticism when an MP protested in the House of Commons that the victor of El Alamein had invited von Thoma, a captured German general, to dinner at his headquarters. "Poor von Thoma," said Churchill drily. "I, too, have dined with Montgomery."

But the legend did him less than justice. Although teetotal himself, his staff and guests never lacked for wine. He loathed tobacco smoke, yet would always hand round cigarettes whenever he stopped to talk to his troops. If he went to bed unusually early it was to be fresh for the next day's decisions—he always rose soon after dawn.

Monty was above all a man of iron

self-discipline, allowing nothing to distract him from his task of winning battles. He was a true leader—dedicated, mindful of his soldiers, utterly straight. Yet the very qualities that gave him such a hold on the hearts and minds of his men made him enemies.

On the Warpath. All too often, breathtaking bluntness and supreme self-confidence bordered on arrogance and egotism. While he could be charming with those of whom he approved, his absolute insistence on efficiency led to officers being sacked with a cold and contemptuous "Useless, quite useless," which rankles in many memories.

Even his most fervent admirers had to acknowledge that he was a prickly, complicated man; but those who knew something of his upbringing were not surprised. It was, as he said himself, a "curious background."

Born in 1887 in a London vicarage, Bernard Law Montgomery was the fourth of the nine children of the future Bishop of Tasmania. He endured a miserably unhappy childhood. His mother often beat him, and many years later he wrote: "A less rigid discipline, and more affectionate understanding, might have wrought better, certainly different, results in me." Repressed at home, Monty sought compensation at school, becoming a fiercely competitive boy with a compulsion to win.

From the Royal Military Academy at Sandhurst he joined the

Warwickshires and spent four years in India. During the First World War he fought in France, survived a rifle bullet through his chest, was awarded the DSO and ended the war a 30-year-old lieutenant-colonel.

To an ambitious young officer in 1918, much seemed wrong with an army whose so-called "good fighting generals" appeared to have been those with the least regard for human life. Monty was to remember this when he, too, became a general, urging his gunnery officers, "If you have 100 tons of shells available and you can save one man's life, then fire the lot." Meanwhile, he determined that if Britain went to war again, "I myself would be prepared, and trained, and ready when the call came."

By the time he was nearing 40, his friends thought him a confirmed bachelor. Then, skiing in Switzerland, he met Betty Carver, an officer's widow. To everyone's surprise, he fell in love. They married in 1927 and, he said, "It had never before seemed possible that such love and affection could exist."

The marriage was the happiest time of his life, and gave him a son, David. But it lasted only ten years before his wife died of blood poisoning. Those who knew him best believed that he never fully recovered: he retreated into his shell, solitary, self-sufficient and totally dedicated to the pursuit of professional excellence.

On the outbreak of the Second World War in 1939 he was a major-general. He acquitted himself so well in France that after the evacuation from Dunkirk he was soon promoted to GOC South Eastern Command, covering Kent, Surrey and Sussex, to organize a mobile system of defence against the expected German invasion. His great opportunity came in August 1942, when he was ordered to Egypt to command the Eighth Army—which included the Seventh Armoured Division, the "desert rats."

He arrived to find morale dangerously low among the men holding the position at El Alamein, to which they had been driven back some 600 miles by the Afrika Korps under Field Marshal Erwin Rommel. To Montgomery the solution to this fundamental problem—restoring the confidence of a dispirited army—was clear. He must become a popular leader.

About Turn. It was an extraordinary performance. Quite deliberately, the solitary, withdrawn Montgomery set out to impress himself on his troops as a personality—human, approachable and, as he put it, "not only a master but a mascot." He bounced around the desert in a jeep, giving pep talks to even the remotest units, dressed in sweater and baggy trousers and sporting the famous floppy black beret with its two cap badges that became his trademark.

The men were inspired by his visits. They warmed to a general who showed a genuine interest in them and lived with them in the desert. They liked his sense of humour: discovering that a tank crew kept a hen called Emma who loyally laid an egg a day, he promoted her to sergeant-major. Passing a lorry driven by a soldier naked except for a top hat, Monty roared with laughter, but decided that a line had to be drawn somewhere, and the order was posted: "Top hats will not be worn in the Eighth Army."

Battle Cry. At home, Winston Churchill was pressing for an offensive in September. But Monty refused to move until he had the firepower and trained manpower to be certain of success. It was at 9.40 p.m. on October 23, 1942, that an artillery barrage of more than 1,000 guns blasted the enemy positions and 1,200 tanks rumbled forward, followed by seven divisions of infantry. Twelve days later the Battle of Alamein had been won, and the German army was in full retreat. As Churchill wrote: "It may almost be said 'Before Alamein we never had a victory. After Alamein we never had a defeat.' "

On May 12, 1943, the Eighth Army having linked up with Anglo-American forces which had landed in Morocco and Algeria, some 248,000 German and Italian soldiers surrendered. The war in Africa was over.

Monty flew home to be knighted by King George VI, and to his astonishment found himself a national figure. Visiting a London theatre in his black beret, he stopped the show. His fan mail reached film-star proportions.

After leading the Eighth Army in the invasion of Sicily and then southern Italy as part of an Anglo-American force under General Eisenhower, Monty was recalled to England for the biggest task of his career: to take command of the Allied armies in what has been called the most complex military operation in history—the Normandy landings.

In a special train code-named "Rapier" he toured Britain, visiting all the troops who were to cross the Channel—British, Canadian, American, Belgian, Polish, Free French, Dutch. These were men grimly expecting to suffer heavy casualties, and he had his own way of putting heart into them.

Marching Orders. He met them at two and often three parades a day, each of some 10,000 soldiers, standing at ease while he walked slowly through the ranks so that they could have a good look at him. Then they gathered round as he told them how, together, they would handle the job. Typically, he asked one guardsman: "What's your most valuable possession?" "My rifle, sir." "No, it isn't," said Monty. "It's your life, and I'm going to save it for you. Listen to me . . ."

The invasion began on June 6, 1944. For Monty, this was a different kind of campaign. In the desert he had fought what was virtually a private war. Now his political masters had agreed that after the invasion and initial battles, he would hand over control to General Eisenhower, the Supreme Commander.

Victory. For almost three months Monty led Anglo-American forces across Normandy, driving the enemy out of France, and was promoted to field marshal. At the triumphant moment of the liberation of Paris, Eisenhower took over. Monty bitterly resented having to step down, believing that if he was allowed to follow up his success he could swiftly end the war with a powerful thrust into Germany itself.

The British and American armies crossed the Rhine and, urged on by Churchill, Monty's 21st Army Group raced for the Baltic coast to seal off the Danish peninsula and prevent Russian forces from occupying Denmark. They made it with six hours to spare. On May 4, 1945, on Lüneburg Heath near Hamburg, Monty accepted the surrender of all German forces in north-west Germany, Denmark and Holland.

Next year he was appointed Chief of the Imperial General Staff, the highest post in the British Army. He was now Viscount Montgomery of Alamein, at 58 a world figure, the seven rows of medal ribbons on his uniform representing honours bestowed by 12 nations.

Following a stormy period in Whitehall as CIGS—"I never minded making myself an infernal nuisance if it produced the desired result," he noted cheerfully—Monty became an international soldier, working once again with General Eisenhower as Deputy Supreme Commander of the NATO forces in Europe. He retired from the Army in 1958 aged almost 71 and promptly embarked on a new way of life, based on Isington Mill, a beautiful old property in Hampshire which he rebuilt after the war with fine timbers presented by Australia and Canada.

Monty became a prolific writer and broadcaster. Television producers found him a natural performer, crisply confident as he re-fought his battles on the small screen. But his favourite activity was travel. He hustled around the world in his self-appointed role as elder statesman with the energy of a man half his age—visiting Russia, India, Central America, Egypt, Canada and China twice, South Africa six times. Always he returned to London in time for the annual Alamein Reunion, the remarkable gathering of desert veterans at which the high point was the entrance of the Eighth Army Commander.

His last foreign trip, in 1967, was a return to the North African battlefields. His friend Denis (now Sir Denis) Hamilton recalls the old man's sombre silence as they walked through the Alamein cemetery commemorating some 20,000 desert soldiers. "When I asked if he would like to visit German and Italian war graves near by, he said: 'I think I've killed enough people without going to see those and be reminded of it.' "

At 79, the desert journey marked the end of his public life. Wrote a small boy the following year: "Dear Sir, I thought you were dead. My father says you are still alive but will die soon. Please send me your autograph quickly." Monty instantly complied, commenting: "I think his approach to the problem was sound."

He spent his last years at home with his memories, re-enacting old campaigns. Recalls the Rev. David Dewing, vicar of the near-by village of Binsted: "Even when he was bedridden, he was still in complete command. Just before Christmas 1975 he said to me, 'When I go, I don't want them to put me in one of those mausoleums in London.' His blue eyes twinkled. 'Do you think you could find me a spot in that churchyard of yours?' "

He died peacefully in his sleep in March 1976. At his funeral, a 19-gun salute thudded across Windsor as six field marshals and the military attachés of 39 countries followed the gun carriage bearing the coffin with the black beret on top to St. George's Chapel. Later that day, Viscount Montgomery of Alamein was laid to rest under a great yew tree in the quiet of Binsted churchyard.

Since then, the visitor's book in the parish church has had to be renewed six times, each fresh volume swiftly filled with signatures as more than 30,000 people from all over the world have come to pay their tribute to the man Sir Brian Horrocks has called the greatest British general since Wellington.

The unsigned message pinned with a single Flanders poppy to a tiny wooden cross at the funeral a year ago spoke for all who lived through the Second World War: "Monty. We will remember you."

ILLUSTRATION: ROGER COLEMAN

First Things First

My 13-year-old daughter and I were talking about women's liberation one day, and I said firmly, "I don't want to be liberated."

My daughter said, "I don't want to be liberated either—at least not until I know how it feels to be captured."　　　　　—Lynn Cannon

Riches Have Wings

Money is a miraculous thing. It is a man's personal energy reduced to portable form and endowed with powers the man himself does not possess. It can go where he cannot go; speak languages he cannot speak; save lives with which he cannot directly deal—so that a man busy all day in an office can at the same time be working in boys' clubs, hospitals and children's centres all over the city.　　　　—Harry Emerson Fosdick

Humour in Uniform

☆☆☆☆☆☆☆☆☆☆☆☆☆☆
☆☆☆☆☆☆☆☆☆☆☆☆☆☆

SIR DAVID ORMSBY GORE, Ambassador to the United States, told this story of his pilot-training days:

"There had been quite a few aircraft taxiing accidents, and the station commander issued a warning that the next pilot causing one would be court-martialled. On the day this warning was issued, I was making a landing with my instructor in the rear seat. As I started my approach, another plane did also, and we finished together, almost in formation. Our planes collided about 15 feet in the air and crashed. No one was injured, but both planes were wrecked. My instructor and I climbed out and stared at the mess for a while. Then he said, 'What good luck! If it had happened ten seconds later, it would have been a taxi accident!'"

—Lieutenant JOHN WILLIAMS

RETURNING G.I. to Statue of Liberty: "Put down that torch, honey. I'm home."   —L. W. MASON

EARLY in 1944 our patrol craft was ordered from Palermo to Naples to give escort support to the Anzio beachhead. About five hours out of Naples, at 2 a.m., a red glow on the horizon brought us to action stations. It might be a torpedoed ship on fire, or perhaps a small naval battle. We proceeded towards the glow at 15 knots—65 men at battle stations, all guns manned, depth charges set, ready for anything. After two hours, the captain asked me as navigator for our position. Imagine my surprise and his embarrassment when I looked along the course line on the chart and saw that we were preparing to attack Vesuvius, then in eruption for the first time for many years!   —E. W. H.

AN X-RAY technician at a medical centre daily processed dozens of bewildered young would-be recruits Each day he would instruct a different group to strip to the waist, line up at the door to the X-ray room and hold out their X-ray cards—and each day someone would hold out the wrong card or go to the wrong door.

One day, after months of the same agonizing ritual, the technician shouted, in a blaze of frustration, "Every day I tell you the same thing! Don't you *ever* learn?" —DONALD LEWIS

AT AN Officer Cadet School in 1956, I was one of 80 raw and apprehensive cadets drawn up in three ranks on the parade ground to be introduced to the senior warrant officer of the school. On marched Regimental Sergeant Major Lynch, Irish Guards, six-foot-three, 16 stone, with gleaming sword and immaculate uniform. He looked as formidable as a tank. Calling us to attention in a voice of thunder and fixing us with a terrifying glare, he said in his Irish brogue, "Gentlemen, let's get one thing straight from the start. I call you 'sir,' and you call me 'sir.' The only difference is, you mean it and I don't!"   —M. R. G.

Mark, the War-Dog Hero

To me he was more
than a friend. He was a true
comrade-in-arms

By John Collings

Lieutenant-colonel "Hoppy" Hopkinson, our commanding officer, delighted in springing surprises. A real martinet, he was determined to keep us on our toes.

One day in December 1939, shortly after the start of the Second World War, when my reconnaissance unit was in north-east France, he sent us on such a gruelling exercise that it was nearly midnight when we tumbled exhausted into our armoured cars. An hour later I was awakened by screams of agony. Dazed, I groped my way outside to find Hoppy scrambling on all fours with Mark, my pet Alsatian, locked to the seat of his breeches. Hoppy had crept towards us along a ditch, expecting to catch us napping—and had been caught by Mark instead.

"Get this ruddy brute off me," Hoppy yelled. As I hurriedly did so, Hoppy, his uniform covered in mud and with a great rent in his breeches, drew himself up and let me have it. "You were all asleep as usual," he stormed.

"Beg your pardon, sir," I replied. "Not all of us." I pointed to Mark, thumping his tail beside me. Hoppy —needing six stitches for his wound —graciously conceded the point.

My friendship with Mark was more than the usual bond between man and dog; we were comrades in arms. I had first seen him a few weeks earlier at Valenciennes, near the Belgian border, when we were stationed with a French unit that trained war dogs. Being a dog lover —I had trained many a champion— I watched admiringly as Mark was put through his paces. Somehow, I determined, he and I would go through the war together.

I sought out the unit's sergeant-major. I wanted Mark badly, I said, and was willing to pay 1,000 francs (at that time about £5·50) for him. The sergeant-major shrugged. "It is not impossible for a dog to slip his chain and run away," he said. I gave him my hotel name and room number, and left it at that.

Three days later I was about to enter my room when my batman cried, "Don't go in, sir. There's a mad dog inside!" I opened the door and there, growling in a corner, stood Mark. Deliberately, I paid no attention to him; I changed for dinner and left.

After dinner, I fetched a big bowl of stew from the kitchen and placed it near Mark along with a bowl of water. Mark refused even to sniff at the food. I undressed and went to bed. During the night he came over to me and sniffed at my hand. Later I heard him drink and then, much later, gobble up his stew. Finally he curled up in his corner and slept.

At six, I dressed and went down to breakfast. When I returned I had a lead in my hand. Now, for the first time, I spoke to Mark, calling his name. Then I bent down and, firmly but unhurriedly, snapped on the lead.

Mark gave no reaction; not even a growl. I stood up, turned my back on him and, calling him, walked to the door. Mark followed obediently at my heel and we set out for the barracks. In my office he curled at my feet while I attended to some papers, and then I took him out on his first parade. So began the career of one of Britain's most famous war dogs—and for me an extraordinary friendship that was to last 13 years.

I continued Mark's tuition, making him familiar with the sound of rifle and mortar fire. Our mobile unit had the task of roaming forward positions and sending information to headquarters. Mark, I saw, could be invaluable for carrying messages and ammunition. He proved an excellent pupil. Soon he could swim a river carrying 200 rounds of ammunition in pouches strapped round his middle, and as a guard dog he was a natural.

On May 10, 1940, the Germans

invaded Belgium and Holland. Against the speed and power of their onslaught, the Allied positions crumpled, and our job of trying to keep track of the chaotic, ever-changing situation left us exhausted. Mark became a hero to my men. Often we were able to snatch some sleep only because Mark was there to guard us. He *never* barked. If there was the slightest suspicious sound or smell he would give a low growl of warning—just enough to alert the sentry.

Mercy Mission. When the Army retreated to the coast, he frequently proved his worth. One evening after heavy fighting in the Flanders plain, six of our men were missing. Attaching a long lead to Mark's collar, I sent him out with my batman to find them. The night was black, but Mark's skill was uncanny. He quickly quartered the area where we had been in action and tracked down two of the men. On Mark's return I sent him out again, this time with a stretcher party; in less than an hour, he guided them safely to the remaining four, who were wounded.

Another night we were holding a position on the Cojeul River. We repulsed several German attempts to cross the river, thanks largely to a machine-gun post I had set up on a small island in midstream with Mark ferrying ammunition to the gunners.

At dawn, I had my field glasses trained on him as he swam back from another trip. Suddenly I saw the water churn up around him as the Germans opened up with a machine-gun. He was hit and started to thrash frantically in the water, but struggled on. When he reached the bank he tried to scramble up, only to slide back exhausted into the water.

Shouting for covering fire, I leaped out of my trench and ran in a crouch to the river. Hanging over the bank, I hauled Mark up by the collar. Then, as I turned to crawl back, I felt a pain shoot up my leg. A bullet had cut through my boot and grazed my anklebone. Hugging Mark against my side, I stumbled to the nearest cover.

My wound was painful but not serious. Mark, though, was in bad shape. The bullet had ripped through his abdomen. When I staunched the blood with an emergency dressing, he took it all without a whimper. Eventually we managed to get back to my car, where I wrapped him carefully in blankets for our trip to a first-aid post.

Ordered to try to get to England on whatever ship was available, we reached Ostend on May 28—the day Belgium surrendered—and filed aboard a British coastal trawler. The ship was crammed with more than 100 men by the time we sailed. Mark lay wrapped in blankets beside me on the deck, too weak to move. Suddenly, out in the Channel, a German E-boat attacked us at almost point-blank range. We fired back with everything we had—Lewis guns, rifles, even revolvers—but before silencing her, we suffered ten dead and about a score wounded.

Next problem: how to smuggle Mark ashore so he wouldn't have to go through the six months' quarantine? My men would have done battle with any official who tried to part Mark from us.

Secret Entry. At Dover I had an idea. The dead were being laid on stretchers and shrouded with groundsheets. I gave Mark a heavy dose of morphine, placed him on a stretcher, and covered him too with a groundsheet. Forming a cortège, we marched down the gangway with our laden stretchers, past the military police and customs men on the quay. A few hours later we were all in London.

I drove to the military hospital at Millbank, looked the medical commandant straight in the eye and said, "Excuse me, sir, but I have a seriously wounded comrade outside." He stared at me as if I were a lunatic.

"Do you like dogs, sir?" I asked, and told him Mark's story. Fortunately, he *did* like dogs. Our wounds were treated, a sample of Mark's blood was taken, and a nurse sent off to the near-by Battersea Dogs' Home. When she returned, Mark was given a much-needed transfusion. Later we were put in the same room together, where we stayed for a couple of weeks.

The army nurses worshipped Mark. Under their care, he recovered so remarkably that during the blitz in early 1941, he gave me one of my happiest memories of him. My wife and I were staying at the Dorchester Hotel, Park Lane, for a weekend. On the Saturday evening, not wanting to leave Mark in our room, I left him with a barman friend and went off to dinner. Later, when we were dancing in the hotel ballroom, I noticed other couples smiling at us. I turned my head—and there was my Alsatian prancing around behind me in step with the music.

For three years I had a military intelligence job which took me all over Britain. During this time, Mark's abilities continued to grow. Once at a training school at Lochailort in the western Highlands, he starred in a number of experiments. A man-size target with a bunch of keys attached was run along a wire stretching the length of a totally dark room. When I aimed a Bren gun so that it pointed in the same direction as the dog's head, and then fired, the target was invariably hit. Why? Because a dog will look directly at the source of a sound, even in complete darkness.

We also tried to find ways of misleading a dog while tracking. We dipped the demonstrator's boots in ammonia, petrol and other chemicals. We even made him wear rubber boots washed in soap and water, which he didn't put on until the moment of setting off. Not one of these ruses succeeded.

In 1944, the year of the Allied invasion of Europe, I took command of a Civil Affairs Unit of Military Government whose job was to follow the troops and restore order. Shortly before D-Day, General Eisenhower visited Beachy Head to inspect invasion troops. As the supreme commander came down the lines, he saw me standing to attention with Mark at my side, his ammunition satchels bearing his wound stripe. Eisenhower stopped and questioned me about Mark's training. Suddenly, he pointed at a near-by army lorry. "Let's see how good a guard your dog is, Major. Put him in that truck over there."

General Alert. I took down the lorry's tail-board, and Mark jumped in. Ike turned to one of his aides. "All right, Butch," he grinned. "See if you can get inside that truck!"

Butch looked pained, but gamely approached the vehicle. As soon as he got within a couple of yards, Mark started to growl and bare his teeth. Butch stopped dead. "Sir," he complained to Eisenhower, "I think I can serve you better alive than dead!"

Ike laughed and said: "That's some dog you've got there, Major."

We landed on the evening of D-Day in the British 50th Division's sector. As we moved up the beach, Mark—just a pace ahead of me—suddenly froze, his ears up and his body on point. I looked carefully at the sand immediately in front of us and could see it had been disturbed. Taking no chances, I called a sapper. Sure enough, there was a mine just below the surface. But for Mark's alertness I might have been killed.

Last Action. Three weeks later, Mark was not so lucky. As we were crossing open country a mine went up in front of us and hurled Mark off his feet. I rushed up and found his right eye was a bloody mess, his right foreleg badly injured. I got him back to a first-aid post, where his wounds were dressed and his leg put in a splint, but nothing could be done about his eye. The optic nerve had gone.

Again Mark made a good recovery. Now blind in one eye and lame, he was no longer much use as a war dog. Still, he contributed to the war effort by taking part in a melodrama at a charity concert in Brussels. He played the faithful dog of a young girl Resistance fighter who had fled with him to her cottage hide-out in the woods. The Germans tracked her down. Suddenly the door burst open and in swept two Nazis. (I had carefully lined their uniforms with protective padding beforehand.) As they leapt forward to arrest the girl, Mark sprang and bowled them over. This was the signal for other Resistance fighters to rush in, bind them up, and rescue the girl.

Mark got a great ovation and

afterwards, as we walked up and down the aisles, people congratulated us and put money into Mark's ammunition pouches—a novel way of collecting a tidy sum for charity.

At the end of the war Mark was awarded his campaign medals, like all other soldiers, and I had the ribbons sewn to his pouches. Eventually we moved to Burgsteinfurt, a pleasant town in Westphalia, where I took up duties as British Resident. Mark enjoyed the peace and comfort, becoming a friend of many Germans. There he died in the summer of 1952. I buried him in the garden of the lovely old house in which I was living. Later some German neighbours put a tablet at the head of his grave. On it was mounted a bronze statue of an Alsatian with the inscription: MARK EIN TREUER FREUND.

On my last day in Germany before retiring from the Army, I went into the garden to pay Mark my final respects. As I looked down at his grave, I thought of the many reasons that will make a man face the dangers and horrors of war: duty, patriotism, belief in a cause, adventure. For a dog, however, it all comes down to one simple thing: love for his master.

Yes, Mark was a true friend. The best I ever had.

ILLUSTRATION: RONALD DUREPOS

Saving Gift

"Do you know what I worry about?" I asked my knowledgeable colleague Max. "Those awkward moments when you feel you have to say something, and you're at a loss for words."

Max smiled. "I never have that problem," he said. "Some years ago, I had the foresight to memorize a suitable list of quotations with which to fill the awkward pauses of my life. For example, at the bus stop I quote Longfellow: 'All things come round to him who will but wait.' After losing a game, I say, 'He that is down needs fear no fall.' Bunyan, you know."

"Max," I said, "surely you must once in a while find yourself with an awkward pause on your hands."

"Never," said Max. "Try me."

"All right," I said. "You are in a lift with an elegantly dressed man on whom you have accidentally spilled your Chinese take-away dinner. As soy sauce runs down his suit, you realize that he looks like an old school chum, but you can't for the life of you recall his name. At that moment your trousers fall down. What do you say?"

"Elementary," said Max, starting to file his nails. " 'Oh wad some Pow'r the giftie gie us, to see oursels as others see us!' Robert Burns."

—H. M.

Project Editor Jo Bourne
Senior Art Editor Conorde Clarke
Designers Sailesh Patel, Chris Francis
Research Assistant Madeline Allen

FOR VIVAT DIRECT
Editorial Director Julian Browne
Art Director Anne-Marie Bulat
Managing Editor Nina Hathway
Trade Books Editor Penny Craig
Picture Resource Manager Sarah Stewart-Richardson
Pre-press Account Manager Dean Russell
Product Production Manager Claudette Bramble
Production Controller Jan Bucil

Origination by FMG
Printed in China

ISBN 978 1 78020 101 6
Book Code 400-580 UP0000-1